Mode 2

Paul Radley • Chris Millerchip

COLLINS E·L·T
London and Glasgow

Collins ELT
8 Grafton Street
London W1X 3LA

© Collins ELT

First published 1989
Reprinted 1989

Designed by Liz Black
Cover illustration by France Chaulet

Typeset in Linotron News Gothic and Novarese by Tradespools Limited, Frome, Somerset, England
Printed in Italy by Canale Spa, Torino

ISBN 0 00 370216 2

This course is accompanied by a Teacher's Book ISBN 0 00 370452 1, a Workbook ISBN 0 00 370451 3 and Cassettes ISBN 0 00 370263 4.

Acknowledgements

The authors would like to thank the following people for their help in the preparation of this book:

Gail Langley, Jan Keane and David Bull, for their advice and suggestions.
Jania Barrell, of Bell Language Institute, London, for her assistance with the recorded materials.
Friends and colleagues at Bell College, Saffron Walden, for their advice and encouragement.

The publishers would like to thank the following for agreeing to participate in recorded interviews and for giving time to be photographed: Jim Leach (27); Sir Richard Attenborough (43); Fionnoula Coulson (59); David Job (75); Michelle Quacoe (91); Denis Lyons (107).

The following also gave time to be photographed: David O'Sullivan and Karen Duffy (8, 12); Helen Stevenson (12); Abigail and Susan Lee (56); Mark Pheeby and Sarah Gardner (60); Scarlett O'Hara (70); Louise Cowel and Alan Daykin (86); Rosemary Kavanagh, Oscie Jolobe, Mark Thompson and Chi Leung (93); Mark Bathurst (94); Bridget Latimer-Jones, Kylie Ferguson and Steven Green (104); Francis Fay and Sarah Allen (110).

The following allowed us to take photographs at their homes or premises: Abigail and Susan Lee (56); The Gap, Regent Street, London (70 – The situation portrayed in the tapescript on this page is entirely fictitious, and no similarity should be inferred between the goods described and those sold by The Gap.).

The publishers are grateful to the following for permission to use original material: Alison Bray, for 'Nice not easy' (10); Tim Madge, for 'The power seekers' (26), 'Message in a bottle' (58) and 'How hard does the royal family work?' (92); Nick Vandome, for 'Angry lesson on freedom' (42); and Martin Waddell, for 'Playing with fire in the north frontier' (106) (these articles appeared originally in the *Guardian*); Uttlesford District Tourist Information Centre, for the map of Saffron Walden (adapted) (22); Cambridge City Council, for the map of part of Cambridge (adapted) (36); Roald Dahl, for the extract from *Poison*, published by Penguin Books in association with Michael Joseph in *Someone Like You* (51); the *Observer*, for the article 'The holiday that's out of this world' by Martin Bailey (66); *Motor Cycle News*, for their advertisement on behalf of Bullet Despatch (89); *Your Amstrad PCW* and Gary Hall, for the advertisement for tuition on the Amstrad 8256/8512 (98); Hills & Dales UK Activity Holidays, for its leaflet (99). The UK area and population chart was adapted from *Encyclopaedia Britannica*, 15th edition (1974), by permission of Enclyclopaedia Britannica Inc. The dictionary entry for the word 'foul' (91) is from the *Collins Cobuild English Language Dictionary*.

The publishers are grateful to the following for the use of photographs: Sporting Pictures (UK) Ltd (6,7); Rex Features Ltd (6,7); Nance Fyson (8, 12, 56, 60, 62, 70, 86, 93, 94, 104, 109, 110); Judy Hallam (24); Paul Radley (24, 27, 43, 59, 75, 91, 105, 107); Network Photographers (26); Ace Photo Agency (28, 67); Allsport (UK) Ltd (31, 73); Barnaby's Picture Library (54); Ann Ronan Picture Library (54); Associated Press (61); EMI (62); Philips Electronics (62); Sony (62); The Photo Source (66); Orion Pictures International (72); All-Action Photographic (72); Simon Warner (74); Janet and Colin Bord (76); Natural History Photographic Agency (77); Oxford Scientific Films (77); Skyscan Balloon Photography (79); Camera Press (92); BBC Enterprises (93); Scottish Television (93); Channel 4 Television (93); British Red Cross (94).

Every effort has been made to contact the owners of copyright material. In some cases this has not been possible. The publishers apologise for any omissions, and will be glad to rectify these when the title is reprinted if details are sent.

Illustrations by Peter Richardson (9, 108, 111), Mark Peppe (16, 32, 33, 48, 49, 64, 65, 80, 81, 96, 112, 113), Jeremy Ford (19, 20, 82, 83, 84, 87, 94, 103, 109), Sharon Gower (29, 38, 39, 57), Kate Charlesworth (30), Iain McIntosh (31, 77), Gary Andrews (45), Ian Kellas (46, 47), Bob Geary (51), Kevin O'Keefe (78) and George Parkin (88, 114).

Maps by Swanston Graphics Ltd (22, 36, 107).
Other artwork by Peter Bull, Jerry Collins and Liz Black.

Contents

PLAN

Unit	Focus	Title	Structures	Functions	Skills
1	Language revision	Fame	Present and past of be Simple present and simple past Present continuous	Exchanging personal information Talking about occupations Describing people	All skills
		Old friends	Simple present Present continuous Simple past Tag questions	Exchanging personal information Talking about what's happening now Talking about the past	All skills
2	Skills	Nice not easy			Reading Listening
		Vocabulary Development Keeping a vocabulary book			
3	Language revision	Plans for Saturday	going to for future Present continuous for future can/can't let's have got to	Talking about future plans Talking about permission Making suggestions Talking about obligation	All skills
		Thief steals £20,000 from finance company	Simple present Simple past Past continuous Prepositions The time	Talking about daily routine Talking about the past Talking about continued past action Describing where things are Talking about the time	All skills
4	Skills	Moondown: Episode 1			Reading Listening
5	Skills	Informal Letters			Writing
	Units 1–5	**Revision Focus**	**Pronunciation (e)**	**Grammar Focus**	
6	Language	Where's the bank?	Imperatives will future	Giving directions	All skills
		Looking at photographs	too/enough with adjectives Indirect statements Modifiers – a bit, very	Expressing opinions Agreeing and disagreeing	All skills
7	Skills	The power seekers			Reading Listening
		Vocabulary Development Noun–adjective links			
8	Language	Break away!	Present perfect Simple past	Talking about experiences	All skills
		Who can cycle faster?	Comparative adverbs	Comparing abilities	All skills
9	Skills	Moondown: Episode 2			Reading Listening
10	Skills	Formal Letters (1)			Writing
	Units 6–10	**Revision Focus**	**Pronunciation (a)**	**Grammar Focus**	
11	Language	Spending habits in Britain	Qualifiers – little, much, few, many, a lot of, plenty of Countable and uncountable nouns	Talking about quantity	All skills
		John Nutting: motorcycle journalist	Present perfect with for and since	Talking about experiences	All skills
12	Skills	Angry lesson on freedom			Reading Listening
		Vocabulary Development Prefixes			
13	Language	War on Want	shall for offers	Making offers	All skills
		The good language student	Modal verbs – must, should, have to, mustn't, shouldn't, don't have to, needn't	Expressing obligation	All skills
14	Skills	Moondown: Episode 3			Reading Listening
15	Skills	Narrating			Writing
	Units 11–15	**Revision Focus**	**Pronunciation (u)**	**Grammar Focus**	
16	Language	Guide to the galaxy	Long numbers	Talking about statistics	All skills
		I used to live in Italy	used to didn't use to did you use to?	Describing previous habits and situations	All skills

Unit	Focus	Title	Structures	Functions	Skills
17	Skills	Message in a bottle Vocabulary Development Synonyms and antonyms			Reading Listening
18	Language	Fed up! The history of hi-fi	too much/many not enough Countable and uncountable nouns Present and past passive	Complaining Talking about processes	All skills All skills
19	Skills	Moondown: Episode 4			Reading Listening
20	Skills	Summaries			Writing
	Units 16–20	Revision Focus	Pronunciation (stress)	Grammar Focus	
21	Language	You've got to do something Madonna	(much) too + adjective Would you mind …? Do you think you could …? Could you …? Relative clauses	Complaining Making polite requests Talking about people, places, things	All skills All skills
22	Skills	The dirty old man of Europe Vocabulary Development Adjective—adverb link			Reading Listening
23	Language	Close encounters Where shall we go?	Modal verbs – must, may, might, can't First conditional	Expressing certainty/ uncertainty Talking about future possibilities (1)	All skills All skills
24	Skills	Moondown: Episode 5			Reading Listening
25	Skills	Reports			Writing
	Units 21–25	Revision Focus	Pronunciation (e)	Grammar Focus	
26	Language	What happened to you? Leave this to me!	Past perfect Reported speech (present)	Talking about an earlier past Reporting what people say	All skills All skills
27	Skills	Fair play for women's football Vocabulary Development Using a monolingual dictionary			Reading Listening
28	Language	The Royal Family First aid	Reported speech (past) Second conditional	Reporting what people said Talking about future possibilities (2)	All skills All skills
29	Skills	Moondown: Episode 6			Reading Listening
30	Skills	Formal Letters (2)			Writing
	Units 26–30	Revision Focus	Pronunciation (ou)	Grammar Focus	
31	Language	Diego Armando Maradona Plans for the end-of-term party	Present perfect continuous with for and since verb + object + infinitive (want, let, make)	Talking about unfinished activities Talking about what you want, are allowed, have to do	All skills All skills
32	Skills	Playing with fire in the north frontier Vocabulary Development Lexical sets			Reading Listening
33	Language Language revision	I wish I looked like Tom Cruise Mistaken identity	wish + past tense Tenses	Wishing	All skills All skills
34	Skills	Moondown: Episode 7			Reading Listening
35	Skills	Compositions			Writing
	Units 31–35	Revision Focus	Pronunciation (r)	Grammar Focus	

NAME: _____
YEAR OF BIRTH: _____
NATIONALITY: _____
COUNTRY OF
RESIDENCE: _____

PROFESSION: _____
AT THE MOMENT: _____
_____
_____

FAMOUS BECAUSE: _____

FAME

Complete the charts with this information.

1952 ~ Irish ~ America ~ Steffi Graf ~
Moroccan ~ training for the Olympics ~
German ~ rock singer ~ athlete ~ training to
remain number one in the world ~ 1970 ~ pop
singer/actress ~ Italy ~ organised the Live-Aid
concert ~ tennis player ~ Germany ~ making a
new record ~ 1959 ~ making TV programmes
about the Third World ~ Said Aouita ~ Bob
Geldof ~ first ten records were number one
hits ~ England ~ set the World 5000 metres
record (1987) ~ American ~ 1960 ~ won the
Wimbledon championship for the first time in
1988 ~ Madonna ~

DO YOU KNOW THESE PEOPLE?

NAME: _____
YEAR OF BIRTH: _____
NATIONALITY: _____
COUNTRY OF
RESIDENCE: _____

PROFESSION: _____
AT THE MOMENT: _____
_____
_____

FAMOUS BECAUSE: _____

NAME: _____
YEAR OF BIRTH: _____
NATIONALITY: _____
COUNTRY OF
RESIDENCE: _____

PROFESSION: _____
AT THE MOMENT: _____
_____
_____

FAMOUS BECAUSE: _____

NAME: _____
YEAR OF BIRTH: _____
NATIONALITY: _____
COUNTRY OF
RESIDENCE: _____

PROFESSION: _____
AT THE MOMENT: _____
_____
_____

FAMOUS BECAUSE: _____

1 Language Focus

Complete these questions.

1 _____ her/his name?
2 When _____ she/he born?
3 _____ she/he from?
4 _____ _____ she/he live?
5 What _____ she/he do?
6 What _____ she/he _____ing now?
7 Why _____ she/he famous?

🎧 1 ▶ **Listen.**

2 *Information check*

Use the same questions. Check the information in your charts with another student.

🎧 2 ▶ **Now listen. Do you and your partner have the right answers?**

3 *Famous people*

1 Guess the famous person!

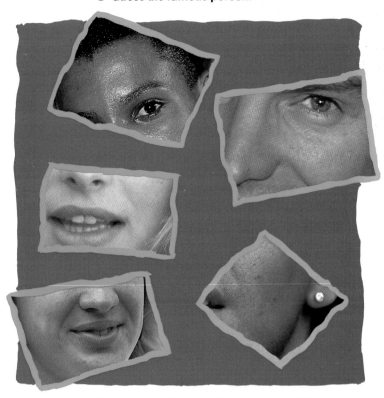

Ask your teacher questions to find out the name of the famous person. You can only ask questions with a 'Yes' or 'No' answer.

Example
Is it a man?
Is he English?

You have a maximum of 10 questions.

2 Read this description of Sylvester Stallone.

Sylvester Stallone is American and was born on July 6th 1946 in New York City. He is an actor–writer and writes the scripts for the popular Rocky films. He also plays the part of Rocky. He is famous as the hero Rambo, too. He's strong and muscular and he's got short dark hair.

Choose one of the famous people from the game. Ask your teacher for more information about the person. Write a description of him/her.

WB 1.1–6

UNIT 1

OLD FRIENDS

🎧 3 ▶ **Cover the dialogue and listen. What do you find out about Robert, Kate and Sandra? Make notes.**

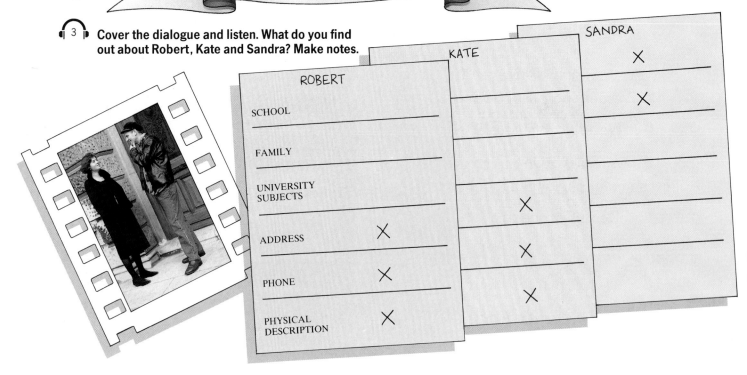

Look at the dialogue and check your answers. Then listen again.

Two students meet outside the university building.

ROBERT Hey! You're Kate Smith, aren't you?
KATE Yes ... But ... Oh, you're not Robert Morris, are you?
ROBERT Yes, that's right. We were at junior school together ... in Stevenage. Do you remember?
KATE Yes, of course. But then we went to live in Leeds.
ROBERT That's right. Your dad works in the police force there, doesn't he?
KATE Mmm. That's right. He's a policeman.
ROBERT And what are you doing now?
KATE I'm at university here in Birmingham.
ROBERT Really? What are you studying?
KATE Chemical engineering. What about you?
ROBERT I'm studying languages: French and Italian.
KATE You've got a brother, haven't you?
ROBERT Yes, that's right ... David. He lives in London now. He's a journalist.
KATE Where do you live?
ROBERT Me? Well ... I'm looking for a flat at the moment.
KATE That's a coincidence! My friend, Sandra, has got a spare room in her flat.
ROBERT What's the address?
KATE 26, New Road. But phone her first.
ROBERT OK. What's her phone number?
KATE 68492.
ROBERT 68492. Great! Is she at university too?
KATE Yes, she's studying biology.
ROBERT What's she like?
KATE She's tall and slim and she's got blue eyes.
ROBERT I see ...
KATE She's really nice!

REVISION FOCUS

STRUCTURES
Simple present
Present continuous
Simple past
Tag questions

FUNCTIONS
Exchanging personal information
Talking about what's happening now
Talking about the past

4 Language Focus

GIRL   You live in Leeds, don't you?
BOY   Yes, that's right.

GIRL   Where did you go to school?
BOY   I went to school in London.

GIRL   What are you doing now?
BOY   I'm studying at the university.

GIRL   You haven't got any brothers or sisters, have you?
BOY   Yes, I've got a brother.

GIRL   What's he like?
BOY   He's tall and slim and he's got brown eyes.

 4 ▶ Listen.

5 Questionnaire

How well do you know your partner? Fill in the missing information, then ask your partner the questions. Check your answers.

NAME	Your name's _____	, isn't it?
AGE	You're _____	, aren't you?
BIRTHDAY	Your birthday's on _____	, isn't it?
ADDRESS	Your address is _____	, isn't it?
PHONE	Your phone number's _____	, isn't it?
BROTHER	You've got _____	, haven't you?
	(You haven't got _____	, have you?)
SISTER	You've got _____	, haven't you?
	(You haven't got _____	, have you?)
PROFESSIONS	Your father's a _____	, isn't he?
	Your mother's a _____	, isn't she?
POSSESSIONS	You've got a _____	, haven't you?
HOLIDAYS	You went to _____	, didn't you?
HOBBIES	You like _____	, don't you?
SINGER	Your favourite singer is _____	, isn't it?
SUBJECT	Your favourite subject is _____	, isn't it?
DAILY ROUTINE	You get up at _____ every morning,	don't you?
SPORTS	You play _____	, don't you?

6 Find your partner!

You are at a party. Ask your teacher to tell you which character you are. Ask questions to find somebody at the party who has three things in common with you.

Tony You're eighteen. You go to school in London. Your favourite subject is French. You've got two sisters. Your father's a teacher. You've got a computer. You like swimming. You play football. You went to France for your holidays.

James You're seventeen. You go to school in Brighton. Your favourite subject is Biology. You've got two sisters. Your father's a taxi driver. You've got a new bike. You like cooking. You play football. You went to Italy for your holidays.

Peter You're eighteen. You go to school in Oxford. Your favourite subject is Biology. You've got a brother and a sister. Your father's a teacher. You've got a new bike. You like reading. You play tennis. You went to Scotland for your holidays.

Sarah You're eighteen. You go to school in Bristol. Your favourite subject is History. You've got a brother and a sister. Your father works in a bank. You've got a TV in your bedroom. You like swimming. You play football. You went to Germany for your holidays.

Julie You're eighteen. You go to school in Cambridge. Your favourite subject is Biology. You've got three sisters. Your father works in a bank. You've got a computer. You like reading. You play basketball. You went to Italy for your holidays.

Kate You're seventeen. You go to school in Bristol. Your favourite subject is Biology. You've got two sisters. Your father's a doctor. You've got a new watch. You like swimming. You play tennis. You went to Spain for your holidays.

WB 1.7–10

1 Skills Focus: Reading

1 Before you read the article, answer these questions.

1 What is an 'au pair'?
2 Would you like to be one?
3 What do you think are the advantages of this kind of work?
4 What are the disadvantages?
5 What sort of household jobs do you think an au pair does?
6 How much do you think an au pair earns each month?
7 Is this sort of work only for girls, in your opinion?

2 Look at the headline of the article by Alison Bray, 'Nice not easy'. Nice is a town in the south of France. Do you think Alison's experience of au pairing was good or bad?

3 Look at the list of jobs. Tick (√) the jobs that you think an au pair usually has to do.

Read the article. Cross (×) the jobs that Alison had to do for the family.

___ ___ wash the children
___ ___ dress the children
___ ___ prepare the dinner
___ ___ prepare the lunch
___ ___ prepare the children for school
___ ___ do the gardening
___ ___ set the table
___ ___ do the shopping
___ ___ vacuum or wash the floors
___ ___ take out and feed the dog
___ ___ wash up the breakfast things
___ ___ prepare the children for bed
___ ___ make breakfast
___ ___ make the beds
___ ___ polish ornaments and wood
___ ___ clean the toilets and bathrooms

4 Find the words and phrases on the left in the text. Match them with their synonyms on the right.

drop everything	type
abroad	consist of
land	stated, said
mould	cooking, cleaning, etc.
stipulated	suddenly stop doing what you are doing
housework	arrive in an aeroplane
involve	legal residence permit
chores	in a foreign country
mounted	boring or unpleasant jobs
day off	sum of money
fee	free day
visa	increased

Nice not easy

Alison Bray takes a spot of French leave

EVERY YEAR thousands of girls from all over the world drop everything in their home country to become au pairs abroad.

A need to improve language skills, discover other cultures, or simply find some independence are the most common reasons, but most have little idea of what is waiting for them.

When I landed in Nice last February, I was as green as the England I left behind. I was to work for a family in the "Nouveau Riche" mould just outside Nice and my contract stipulated caring for the children and "petite aide menagere" (light housework).

I found, in fact, all the house work in the large villa was my responsibility.

A typical morning's work would involve washing and dressing the five-, seven — and nine-year-old children, preparing them for school, washing up the breakfast things, making the beds (to army standards), tidying their rooms and play rooms, cleaning and making the fire, vacuuming and washing either the upstairs or downstairs floor surfaces, polishing ornaments and all wood, cleaning the toilets and bathrooms, taking out and feed-ing the dog, setting the table and preparing part of the lunch.

The chores steadily mounted each week, so was usually working from a.m. until 9 p.m. with a two hour break after lunch, six days a week, for £140 month.

Despite Mme. H. agree-ing on my contract that would have "une vie de familie," I could not eat with out her permission (she even locked away some things). had to drink cheap sterilised milk rather than their "biological" milk and was left work on my day off.

She would not wash my black or coloured clothes, was refused a key, and only allowed one evening off week ... if I returned by 10 p.m.

Talking to other girls, was convinced this was not right. After six weeks I an-nounced I was going. Neither my agency in England nor Nice was ever of any help.

The agent in Nice, at one stage, threatened me, believing my employer in preference to me: not sur-prising as they collected a nice fee for each new girl introduced.

I found my last family through a friend and spent three very happy months with them, living above their patisserie.

If you want to au pair it is worthwhile using an agency if only to have the chance of meeting others through a language school, which they organise.

Some countries require a visa.

And, by the way, boys have been known to work as au pairs.

From the *Guardian*, 2 December 1987

5 True or false?

1 Most people go abroad to be au pairs.
2 The family lived in the centre of Nice.
3 There were three children in the family.
4 Alison had to work twelve hours a day, seven days a week.
5 Alison changed families after about six weeks.
6 The second family was not very kind.
7 Most au pairs are girls.

2 *Skills Focus*: Listening

Paul is at the Bees Knees au pair agency in Kew. He's talking to an employee of the agency about the work.

 1 Listen. Which of these questions does Paul ask the woman? Put a tick (√).

____ How many au pairs do you employ?
____ How many employees have you got at the agency?
____ How old are your au pairs?
____ Where do they usually come from?
____ Do you have any au pairs from the United States?
____ Do you ever employ men or boys as au pairs?
____ What sort of qualities do you look for in a good au pair?
____ Do you ever have any problems with your au pairs?
____ How many au pairs leave before the end of their contract?
____ How long do they usually stay?
____ What sort of conditions do you offer your au pairs?

 2 Listen again and make notes about the woman's answers to Paul's questions.

3 Discuss in groups.
What do you think of the conditions that the agency is offering? Are they fair in your opinion? Think about

the money the au pairs get
the hours they work
their evening duties
conditions of board and lodging.

3 *Vocabulary Development*

Keeping a vocabulary book
Create your own vocabulary book and help yourself to be more organised in your study. It will help you to learn more efficiently. You can decide yourself the best way of organising it. Below you will see several examples of layout. Decide which is most suitable for you.

1 You can take a plain exercise book and leave a section for each unit of the textbook. In each section put the new words you meet in that unit and also any other words that are linked in any way. You will see examples of this kind of vocabulary development in later sections.

2 You can keep a file for your study notes with vocabulary in one section.

3 You can list your vocabulary in an alphabetical notebook.

PLANS FOR SATURDAY

🎧 6 ▷ **1 Cover the dialogue and listen. Make notes under these headings.**

1 Robert's plans for Saturday
2 Kate's plans for Saturday
3 What Sandra's got to do on Saturday

2 Look at the dialogue and check your answers. Then listen again.

KATE   So, what are you doing on Saturday, Robert?

ROBERT Well, I'm going to buy a birthday present for Pete in the morning. It's his eighteenth birthday next week.

KATE   What are you going to buy him?

ROBERT I'm not sure. I'd like to get him a compact disc but they're so expensive.

KATE   I'm going into town on Saturday morning, too. Let's meet for lunch.

ROBERT That's a good idea. We can go to that new hamburger place in the High Street.

KATE   Great! And then in the afternoon I'm going to the cinema. Why don't you come, too?

ROBERT Thanks. I'd love to. And then to finish the day let's go to a club.

Kate's friend, Sandra, arrives.

KATE   Hi, Sandra. We're having lunch in town on Saturday, then we're going to the cinema and to a club in the evening. Why don't you come?

SANDRA No, I can't, Kate. I've got to go to the dentist in the morning and then we're going to Grandma's for lunch. And I can't go to the club because Auntie Jane and Uncle Jim are coming to dinner and I've got to talk to my cousin, Nigel.

KATE   Nigel! Oh, no. You poor thing! He's so boring.

SANDRA There's nothing I can do about it, Kate. Hey, Robert. Why don't you come to dinner on Saturday, too?

ROBERT Sorry, I can't. I'm going to the club! I think it's going to be more fun than dinner with your cousin, Nigel!

REVISION FOCUS

STRUCTURES

going to for future
Present continuous for future
can/can't
let's
have got to

FUNCTIONS

Talking about future plans
Talking about permission
Making suggestions
Talking about obligation

1 Language Focus

KATE So, what are you doing on Saturday, Robert?
ROBERT I'm going to buy a birthday present.
KATE Let's meet for lunch.
KATE We're having lunch in town on Saturday.
SANDRA I can't go to the club.
SANDRA I've got to go to the dentist.

 Listen.

RULES AT HOME

	YOU	YOUR PARTNER
1 Do you have to help in the house?		
2 Can you smoke at home?		
3 Can you drink alcohol?		
4 Are you going to leave home as soon as possible?		
5 Do you have to tidy your room?		
6 Are you going to look after your parents when they're old?		
7 Can you invite your friends home?		
8 Can you watch the TV programmes you want to?		
9 Can you stay out after 11 p.m.?		
10 Can you go to discos?		
11 Do your parents want to know where you're going when you go out?		
12 Do your parents give you money to spend?		
13 Can you choose your own clothes?		
14 Can you go on holiday with your friends?		

2 Roleplay

1 Work in groups of three—Student A, Student B and Student C. Have a conversation.

STUDENT A You are going to London on Saturday.
Morning : British museum
Afternoon: Shopping to buy a pair of shoes
Evening : Theatre
Tell B your plans for Saturday.
Invite B to go shopping with you and to the Theatre
Invite C.
Refuse C's invitation for the evening and give your reason.

STUDENT B You are going to London on Saturday.
Morning : Visit aunt in Hospital
Afternoon: Shopping to buy a pair of jeans
Evening : Don't know
Tell A your plans for Saturday
Accept A's invitations for the afternoon and evening.
Refuse C's invitation for the evening and give your reason

STUDENT C
Morning : You've got to work at the university.
Afternoon: Visit grandparents
Evening : Party at Steve's house
You don't like steve but you've got to go.
Invite A and B to go to the party with you.

2 Work with your group and write the conversation you had.

3 Questionnaire

1 Read the questionnaire.

Write your answers in the column YOU. Ask your partner the questions and put his/her answers in the second column.

Here are some possible answers.

Yes.   No.   I think so.   I hope so.
Yes, sometimes.   I'm not sure.

2 Write a paragraph comparing what you can do with what your partner can do. Begin like this:

I have to help in the house every day but Giovanni only has to help sometimes.

WB 3.1–3

Thief steals £20,000 from finance company

Police are investigating the theft of £20,000 from the safe of the famous finance company, Grabbit and Run, in the centre of London yesterday. The director of the company discovered the theft at 12.30 yesterday, a time when several employees were out of the office at lunch. The police suspect that the thief works for the company. Mr Grabbit, who owns the company, was in Paris for a conference at the time of the theft. He will arrive back in London this afternoon. He is shocked and upset at what has happened.

'I can't believe that it was one of my employees,' he said when interviewed at his hotel. 'They are a pleasant, hardworking group of people and I have always had complete trust in them.

REVISION FOCUS

STRUCTURES

Simple present
Simple past
Past continuous
Prepositions
The time

FUNCTIONS

Talking about daily routine
Talking about the past
Talking about a continued action in the past
Describing where things are
Talking about the time

True or false?

1 A thief stole the money from the bank.
2 Mr Grabbit is the director of the company.
3 The director of the company doesn't have lunch between 12 o'clock and 1 o'clock.
4 Mr Grabbit was in France on holiday.
5 Mr Grabbit suspects one of his employees.

4 *Language Focus*

What does Betty do at the company?
What time does Delia start work?
What time does Frank have lunch?
What time does Eric finish work?
Where's Colin's office?
Has Alice got the keys to the safe?
What was Eric doing from 12 o'clock to 1 o'clock?

 8 **Listen.**

UNIT 3

5 Identify the thief

Work in groups of three – Student A, Student B and Student C.

Read your paragraph about the people at Grabbit and Run. Fill in the information you have on the chart and the plan.

Ask the other two people in your group questions like the ones in the Language Focus to find out the rest of the information.

The first person to identify the thief is the winner.

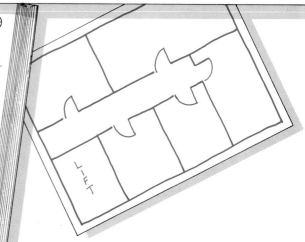

MAIN STREET POLICE STATION

Name: _____

Job: _____

Work timetable
Starts work: _____

Has lunch: _____

Finishes work: _____

Position of office: _____

Keys to safe: _____

Other relevant information: _____

STUDENT A

Alice and Colin start work at 9 o'clock and finish at 5 o'clock but Frank starts work at 9.15 and finishes at 5.15. Colin is the company's accountant. Betty is Alice's secretary, so she works in Alice's office. Colin has got keys to the safe but Delia and Frank haven't. Colin's office is next to Eric's. Betty has lunch from 1 o'clock to 2 o'clock. On the day of the theft Frank went to a restaurant for lunch with Eric. Alice was phoning her sister from 12 o'clock to 12.30. Alice discovered the theft at 12.30.

STUDENT B

Alice is the director of the finance company. There are five people who work with her, Betty, Colin, Delia, Eric and Frank. Eric starts work at 8.45 and finishes work at 4.45. Eric is the sales manager of the company. He has lunch at 12 o'clock, and Delia has lunch at 12 o'clock, too, while Alice has lunch at 1 o'clock. Alice has keys to the safe. The safe is in Eric's office. Eric's office is opposite Alice's office. Delia's office is opposite the lift and next to Alice's office. Betty was out of the office from 12.10 to 12.20 when she went to buy a newspaper.

STUDENT C

Betty starts work at 9.15 and finishes work at 5.15. Delia starts work at 8.45 and finishes work at 4.45. Delia is advertising manager in the company. Frank has lunch from 12 o'clock to 1 o'clock, and Colin has lunch from 1 o'clock to 2 o'clock. Betty and Eric have keys to the safe. Frank's office is between Eric's office and the lift. Frank is the company's post boy. Eric was twenty minutes late for work on the day of the theft. While Alice was phoning her sister her office door was closed. Delia saw Betty leave the office at 12.10 (she was having lunch in the pub opposite the entrance to the office). On the day of the theft Eric was at lunch with Frank from 12 o'clock to 1 o'clock.

6 Alibis

Read the instructions carefully.

1 Someone killed a policeman in your town last Saturday night at 9 o'clock. The police suspect a member of the class of the murder.

2 The suspect and another person in the class leave the room for five minutes and prepare an alibi for themselves for Saturday night between 7 o'clock and 10 o'clock.

3 While the two students are outside, the rest of the class prepare questions to ask them about their alibi.

4 One of the students comes back into the room. The class ask the student their questions about Saturday night and make notes.

5 The second student comes back into the room and the class ask the same questions. If two or more of the answers are different, the suspected student is guilty!

WB 3.4–6

MOONDOWN

Skills Focus: Reading and Listening

1 Read the episode quickly and answer these questions.

1 What type of story is this going to be (science fiction, comedy, thriller, spy story)?
2 What are the names of the principal characters and what do they do?
3 What is Moondown and where is it?

 9 **Now listen and read the episode again.**

EPISODE ONE

Cathy Edwards is a reporter for the *Westfield Gazette*, the local newspaper of Westfield, a small town on the East Anglian coast. Pete Chisman works as a photographer for the same newspaper. It's Friday afternoon and Cathy and Pete are in Cathy's office.

'This is an interesting article, Pete. Have you read it?'

'Which article?'

'This one in the *National Guardian*. It's about the effects of dumping nuclear waste in the sea.'

'Oh, that one ...'

'Well, have you read it?'

'No, I haven't, Cathy. I'm not really interested in it.'

'Why not? Nuclear energy is a problem which should interest us all!'

'Why?'

'Well, radioactive material can cause all sorts of health problems ...'

'For example?'

'Cancer, for example. It says here that in the village of El Garbo in Northern Spain the incidence of cancer has risen by 40 per cent in the last ten years. They built the first nuclear power station in that area fifteen years ago!'

'OK, I'm interested now. Let me have a look, then.'

'Here you are.'

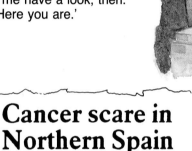

Cancer scare in Northern Spain

from our Spanish correspondent

THE people of El Garbo, a fishing village in the north west of Spain, are protesting about poor safety regulations at the local nuclear power station. A survey has shown that there has been a 40 per cent increase in the cases of cancer in the area in the last ten years.

The power station at El Garbo was opened fifteen years ago and doctors fear that the significant increase in the number of cancer cases is related to the practice of dumping nuclear waste in the sea off the coast near El Garbo.

The main industry in El Garbo, apart from tourism, is fishing, and it is feared that fish caught locally may have been contaminated by radioactive waste.

Government health officials say that the level of radioactivity in the sea is 'below the established EEC danger level' but the people of El Garbo are asking for a government enquiry into the matter.

'Mmm ... Sounds serious! It'll be interesting to see what happens at the enquiry.'

'If there *is* an enquiry! I wonder what they do with nuclear waste at Moondown power station.'

'Yes, me too, Cathy ... and Westfield's on the sea, just like El Garbo ... *and* the main industry is fishing!'

'Anyway, it's no good worrying. Come on, it's five o'clock, time to go home. See you on Monday, Pete!'

'Yes. Have a good weekend, Cathy.'

2 Write the line number of these words from the newspaper article about Northern Spain.

Example

scare ___1___

increase ___   waste ___   main ___   below ___

dumping ___   power station ___   fear ___   off ___

danger ___   matter ___   poor ___

Now put the same words into these sentences.

1 The car nearly hit Robert and gave him a bad _____ .
2 One of the worst forms of pollution is the _____ of rubbish at the side of the road and on the banks of rivers.
3 Last year there were 16 people in my class; this year there are 20. This is an _____ of 25 per cent.
4 The temperature is −5°C today, that is 5° _____ 0°.
5 Richard's _____ interest is fishing; in fact he goes fishing five times a week.
6 _____s produce electricity.
7 Nuclear _____ is the radioactive material which remains after the production of nuclear energy.
8 The island of Capri is one mile _____ the coast near Sorrento.
9 People who smoke cigarettes are in _____ of getting cancer.
10 At the time of the Chernobyl disaster European politicians discussed the _____ in the European parliament.
11 Attendance at the meeting was very _____ ; only three people came.
12 Six people died in the accident but police _____ that more people will die as the result of injuries.

Check your answers with another student.

3 Answer these questions.

1 Which newspaper do Cathy and Pete work for?
2 What day is it?
3 Where are Cathy and Pete?
4 What is Cathy doing?
5 Is Pete interested in the article?
6 What is the article about?
7 Why does Cathy get angry?
8 Is Pete interested in the problem when he finishes the article?
9 What are the similarities between El Garbo and Westfield?

4 True or false?

1 El Garbo is on the south coast of Spain.

2 The villagers want better safety regulations at the local power station.
3 More people have got cancer in El Garbo than had it ten years ago.
4 Nuclear waste from the power station has probably caused the increase in cancer.
5 The only industry in El Garbo is fishing.
6 Nuclear waste in the sea has contaminated the fish with radioactivity.
7 Government officials say that the situation is very dangerous.
8 The people of El Garbo believe the health officials.

5 Read these statements.

1 On Saturday morning
a Pete phones Cathy.
b Cathy phones Pete.
c Pete is at Cathy's house.

2 Pete is surprised because
a Cathy wants to meet him.
b it's very early.
c Cathy is excited.

3 They arrange to meet
a in half an hour.
b in an hour.
c in ten minutes.

4 Someone came to Cathy's house and
a left a letter.
b gave her a letter.
c opened her door.

5 The letter is about
a Cathy's newspaper.
b a trip to Westfield.
c Moondown power station.

6 The writer of the letter is
a anonymous.
b a friend of Cathy.
c a newspaper reporter.

7 What is Pete's attitude to the letter?
a Sceptical.
b Excited.
c Worried.

8 What does Cathy intend to do on Monday morning?
a Go to the police.
b Talk to the editor of the *Westfield Gazette*.
c Nothing.

 Listen to the conversation between Cathy and Pete. Tick the correct answers.

WB 4

UNIT 5

Skills Focus: Writing Informal Letters

Read the letter and notes.

House number before street name.

Address and date but not your name.

Date can also be *August 30th, 1988* or *30/8/88.*

16, Willerton Road,
Southampton,
SO9 1BE.
30ᵗʰ August 1988

Standard beginning for all letters.

Begin letter with a capital.

Dear Emma,
          Thank you for your letter. It was good to hear from you. I'm glad you had a good holiday. We went to Scotland in August and had a lovely time. First we went to the Edinburgh Festival and saw some very interesting shows. Then we went camping in the Highlands. It was fantastic but the weather wasn't very good. We went for some long walks and we went swimming in the lakes but the water was freezing.

Paragraphs can be indented or not, but be consistent.

An informal letter is like spoken language so you can use short forms, e.g. *I'm, he's.*

          At the moment I'm doing a lot of work for school. It's really difficult at the end of the holidays but I've got a lot to do before school starts next week. We've got a new Maths teacher this year. He's very strict and gives a lot of homework. I don't think I'll do very well in Maths this year!

          I'm really looking forward to seeing you again. Why don't you come to Southampton for a weekend? I'm having a party on September 5ᵗʰ and it would be lovely to see you. I bought a couple of Madonna records during the holidays and I'm sure you'll like them. Try and come. Ring me and let me know.
          Give my love to your parents and Jim.
See you soon, I hope.
                    Love,
                         Mary

Friendly ending.

Useful phrases for

a beginning your letter
Thank you for your letter …
It was lovely to get your letter yesterday …
I'm sorry I didn't write earlier but …

b general news
I went to …
Did you know that …?
I'm going to …

c ending your letter
Hope to hear from you soon.
Please write and tell me …
Thank you again for …

d last words before your signature
Yours,
Love,
Lots of love,

Write a similar letter to a friend. Make sure that you put your address and the date at the top of the letter.

Paragraph one Talk about your summer holidays. Say where you went and describe some of the things you did.

Paragraph two Talk about the new term at school. Describe a new teacher or a new student in the class.

Paragraph three Invite your friend to do something with you next weekend. End your letter.

WB 5

18

REVISION FOCUS

1 Days of the week

What days of the week are these dates this year?

1 September 14th

_____

2 September 30th

_____

3 September 19th

_____

4 September 8th

_____

5 September 3rd

_____

6 September 25th

_____

7 September 27th

_____

2 Food and drink

Can you find 14 things to eat or drink? You can read across and down.

```
C A K E P E A R G T S
O P S G O D S I R E W
B P C G T M E A T A E
L L O C A B R E A D E
F E F O T E W K P F T
O S F K O E L E M O N
S O E E N R I B I P A
T U E Y G R A N L E G
E W A T E R D R K T U
```

3 Furniture

What are these items of furniture?

Example
It's made of wood.
You sit on it.
Chair.

1 It's made of wood or metal.
You sleep on it.

_____

2 It's made of wood.
It's sometimes square, sometimes round and sometimes oval.

_____

3 You can put it on the table or on the floor.
It helps you to see better in the evening.

_____

4 It's in the kitchen.
It's very cold inside.

_____

5 It's sometimes in the living room and sometimes in the bedroom.
You put books in it.

_____

6 It's often on the wall.
You can tell the time by it.

_____

7 It's usually in the living room.
It shows pictures either in colour or in black and white.

_____

8 It has two doors.
You put your clothes in it.

_____

9 You often have it on your desk.
It's useful when you do maths.

_____

10 It's often on the wall.
When you look at it, you see yourself.

_____

4 Clothes

Write down the names of the clothes you can see in the wardrobe.

19

5 Illnesses

What's wrong with these people?

6 Sports

Look at the picture. How many sports can you find?

7 Functions

🎧 11 **Look at the functions and listen to the exchanges on tape. Write the number of each exchange next to its function.**

_3_ Describing people

___ Giving personal information

___ Talking about the past

___ Talking about future plans

___ Making suggestions

___ Talking about obligation

___ Talking about permission

___ Talking about daily routine

___ Describing where things are

8 Verb tenses

Complete the paragraph about Barbara's disastrous holiday. Put in the verbs in the correct tense.

Barbara Davies _____ in London with her parents and her brother, Edward.

Barbara _____ eighteen years old and she _____ to university in London. Edward _____ twenty-two years old and at the moment he _____ in a bank but he _____ it very much. Last year he _____ an old car and he and Barbara _____ on holiday together. The holiday _____ a disaster! They _____ on camp sites but the weather _____ awful: it _____ every day! Then they _____ an accident when they _____ along the motorway but fortunately it _____ serious. They _____ very glad to get home!

🎧 12 9 Pronunciation

Look at these words.

1 delicious   2 centre

Listen and repeat. Listen especially to the pronunciation of the letter _e_ in the first syllable of each word.

Now look at these words and decide which category they belong to. Write _1_ or _2_.

before ___	remember ___
seven ___	plenty ___
English ___	prepare ___
return ___	preparation ___
remind ___	every ___
terrible ___	decide ___
excellent ___	believe ___

Listen and check your answers.

GRAMMAR FOCUS

Read the sentences and complete the chart.

1 He's from London.
2 I'm playing tennis on Saturday.
3 They're staying at the Richmond Hotel this week.
4 We went to Scotland last summer.
5 He was walking down the street when the accident happened.
6 I'm going to work in a bank (when I leave school).
7 People will travel by personal helicopter in the year 2000.
8 He's got a walkman and a calculator.
9 I've got to do the shopping this afternoon.
10 Can I go to the concert, please?
11 He can swim very fast.

SENTENCE NUMBER	STRUCTURE	FUNCTION
9	'have got to' + infinitive ('do')	Talking about obligation
_____	_____	Talking about ability
_____	_____	Making predictions
_____	_____	Talking about the present situation
_____	_____	Talking about personal information
_____	_____	Describing simultaneous actions in the past
_____	_____	Talking about future arrangements
_____	_____	Talking about possessions
_____	_____	Talking about the past
_____	_____	Asking permission
_____	_____	Talking about future intentions

In these units you have revised

the simple present
the present continuous
the simple past
the past continuous
tag questions
going to for future
the present continuous for future
can/can't
let's
have got to
prepositions
the time.

Check that you know these things before you go on to the next unit.

UNIT 6

Where's the bank?

1 Before you listen, discuss these questions.

1 Do you always understand the directions people give you in your own language?
2 Do people always give precise directions?
3 Do you ask people to repeat them?
4 Do you often ask someone else?
5 How do you feel about giving directions?
6 Do you often give directions?
7 How do you guide people?
8 Do you use landmarks?

13 2 Listen and answer these questions.

1 Which three places does Sinan visit?
2 Does he get what he wants?
3 Does he manage to send something to his sister?

13 3 Listen again.

1 Mark the three places Sinan visits.
2 Mark any landmarks that people give Sinan.

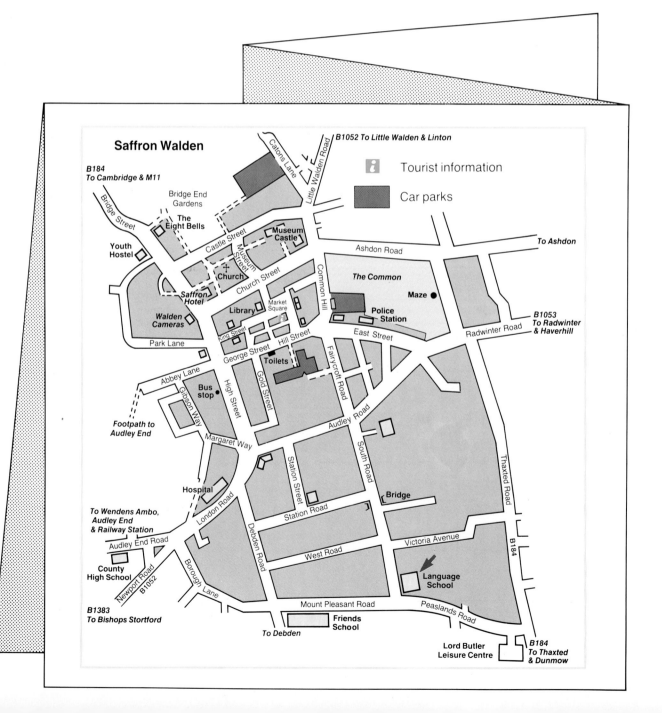

22

1 Language Focus

🎧 14 🎧 **1 Listen to and read this conversation. Mark the two pubs, The Railway (R) and The Duke of York (D), and also the Indian restaurant (I), on the map. John is coming out of the language school in South Road.**

JOHN Excuse me. Is there an Indian restaurant near here?

MAN Sorry, I'm a visitor here.

JOHN Oh ... thanks, anyway. Er ... excuse me. Is there an Indian restaurant near here?

WOMAN Yes, there is. You go down South Road and take the second left, after the bridge. Take the first right. There's a pub on the corner called The Railway. Go down to the end of that road. Turn left at the end and the Indian restaurant's about 50 metres down that road, on the left. It's just after a pub called The Duke of York.

JOHN So that's second left, first right, left again and it's on the left after about 50 metres.

WOMAN That's right.

JOHN Thanks very much.

2 Complete this conversation.

ANNIE Is there a good hotel in Saffron Walden?

MAN Yes, _____ Saffron Hotel.

ANNIE _____ that?

MAN Well, you _____ down South Road and _____ left after the bridge. Go straight _____ Station Road and _____ right at the end. You're in _____ Road, then London Road. Go _____ down London Road and after 50 metres it turns into High Street. You'll see the Post Office on your _____.

ANNIE OK, got that.

MAN The Saffron Hotel is about 100 _____ on your _____ after the _____.

ANNIE I think I can remember that. _____ very much.

🎧 15 🎧 **Listen and check your answers, then practise the conversation in pairs.**

Now cover the dialogue. Look at the map and practise the conversation again.

3 Work in pairs. Give directions to get from the language school to these places on the map. Mention at least two landmarks in your directions.

1 the castle
2 the museum
3 the hospital
4 the youth hostel
5 the County High School

2 Where do you live?

Imagine that you live in Saffron Walden. Choose an address. Mark your house on the map.

Give directions to get to your house from the bus stop in High Street.

Ask three other students for directions to get to their houses. Mark the locations of their houses on your map.

3 Helping a visitor

1 Work in pairs.

Student A **Imagine you are a visitor to your town. Ask Student B for directions from your school to**
the station
the library
a bank.

Student B **Give Student A directions. When you finish change roles and ask Student A for directions from your school to**
the post office
a swimming pool
a good record shop.

🎧 16 🎧 **2 Barbara is at the car park on the common. She is asking for directions to two places in Saffron Walden. Follow the directions and tick the names of the places.**

Bridge End Gardens ____

youth hostel ____

post office ____

Friends School ____

library ____

The Eight Bells pub ____

church ____

Walden Cameras ____

police station ____

WB 6.1–4

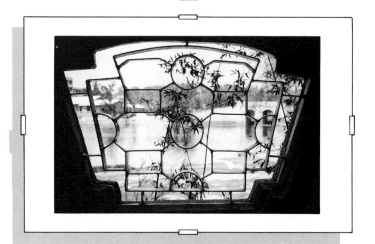

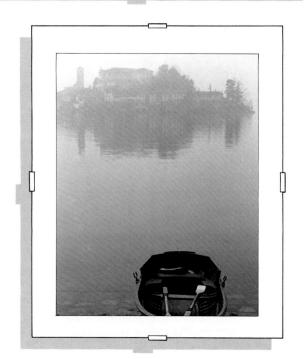

LOOKING AT PHOTOGRAPHS

🎧 17 ▶ **Look at the photographs and listen. Jan and Bruce are at a photographic exhibition.**

Now answer the questions.

1 Which three photos are they talking about? Put ticks (√).
2 Why doesn't Bruce like the first photo?
3 Is Jan's opinion the same?
4 What does Bruce say about the photo with the river?
5 Which photo do they both like?

6

24

UNIT 6

4 Language Focus

Complete the dialogues.

A _____ do you _____ of this _____ ?

B Which _____ ?

A The _____ with the old man and the trees.

B I _____ it's beautiful.

A Yes, I agree with you. I _____ it's very good.

C _____ do you _____ of this _____ ?

D Which _____ ?

C The _____ of the _____ singing.

D I don't _____ it. I _____ _____ it's clear enough.

C Oh, I _____ _____ with you. I _____ it's nice.

🎧 18 **Now listen and check your answers.**

5 Discuss the photographs

Look at the photographs. Write down either a positive or a negative adjective for each one.

Now discuss the photographs with another student.

Example

STUDENT A What do you think of this one?
STUDENT B Which one?
STUDENT A The one of the old car.
STUDENT B I think it's very good.
STUDENT A I agree with you. I think it's good too.

When you finish, discuss the photographs with another student. Try to find a student with the same opinion as you.

6 What's your opinion?

1 Work in groups.

Which photograph would you like to put on the wall of your classroom? Discuss the photographs and choose one that you all like.

2 Look at the paragraph that Jan wrote in her diary about the photographic exhibition. Write a similar paragraph about your favourite photograph. Describe the photograph and say why you like it.

May
30 Saturday

Today I went to a photographic exhibition with Bruce. I enjoyed it very much. My favourite photograph at the exhibition is of a man singing. I think the man is a rock singer. He's black and he's wearing glasses and he looks American.

May

He's got a microphone in his left hand and he's holding his right hand next to his ear. I think the photograph is very good because it's very simple but quite dramatic.

WB 6.5–7

25

The power seekers

What do young people think about nuclear power? Young Guardian asked some to visit Sizewell

by Tim Madge

PARLIAMENT next week debate the Layfield Report which has said the second Sizewell nuclear reactor — Sizewell "B" — should be built. But the controversy over the idea of building any more nuclear power stations is unlikely to die down.

The Central Electricity Generating Board believes that it is lack of information among the public that has led to the negative attitudes many people now have. Young Guardian took a party of youngsters — aged from 14-17, — on a visit to the CEGB nuclear power station at Sizewell in the week in January the Layfield report was published. This is their report.

"I WAS DETERMINED to go in with an unbiased opinion," said Elizabeth Abrahams (16), a view echoed by most of her seven companions, all from Billericay School in Essex.

Their first view of the installation was across the fields and hedgerows of a wintry Suffolk landscape, brilliantly lit by a clear blue sky. "A large clump of trees desperately tried to hide the huge white buildings," said Elizabeth. "Everything looked so peaceful — it was hard to imagine the place had the potential to be dangerous."

Katie Nibbs (14) said: "The day began with a highly simplified explanation of how nuclear power operates — descriptions like 'glorified kettle' and the 'object of all this controversy is boiling water,' were perhaps meant to set our minds at rest."

Kala Subbuswany (14) added: "The power station was clean and the people friendly but I couldn't help feeling like a customer who had been subjected to a lengthy sales talk — the salesman — the CEGB, the product — nuclear power."

The three boys were more certain that nuclear power was safe and necessary. "I left Billericay with an open mind," said 14-year-old Ian Hammond. "I came away feeling I was for nuclear energy."

Zafar Sarfraz (17) agreed: "I must admit Sizewell 'A' impressed me greatly. We took around a device to measure radiation — all the levels were harmless. I still believe, though, the major problem is the handling and disposal of radioactive waste."

David Thomas said he too had been dubious about safety before he went but "the managers we talked to thought the most dangerous part of their jobs was driving to and from work. I think public concern stems from lack of knowledge."

The group were able to tour the plant, including the reactor building, and later closely questioned Sizewell staff about all the aspects of safety and radioactive waste — the two main issues that bothered them.

Collette Gilmore (16), while impressed by the replies, was still worried: "I was dubious about safety and in the end I was not convinced of the need for nuclear power. In about ten years Sizewell will have to be shut down at great cost — the waste disposal question is unanswered."

Katie continued: "The nuclear inspectorate (who look after safety matters in the public's name) are not present at every stage of construction and operation. Accidents that theoretically cannot happen in practice do."

Everyone asked repeatedly about Chernobyl. "The place looked so picturesque and yet some hidden fear nagged incessantly at the back of my mind," said Elizabeth. And Kala agreed: "Everyone said a serious accident could never happen here. Before Chernobyl the Soviets said the same."

The visit did show one thing: more publicly available information about nuclear power is still needed. The tour helped but for some it was not good enough. They had not seen everything —like the cooling ponds where the waste is temporarily stored — and it bothered them. Although one or two minds were changed — among the boys — for the rest the doubts lingered on.

All nuclear power stations in England and Wales allow visitors and hold open days.

From the *Guardian*, 18 February 1987

1 Skills Focus: Reading

1 In groups, make a list of all the vocabulary you know which has to do with nuclear energy.

2 Before you read the text, discuss these questions.

1 Is nuclear power necessary, in your opinion?
2 What are the alternatives?
3 Would you like to live near a nuclear power station?
4 Imagine you are visiting a nuclear power station. What questions about nuclear power stations do you want to ask?

3 Look for this information while you read the text for the first time.

1 The number of young people who visited Sizewell.
2 The name of their school.
3 The two problems which interested the visitors most.

4 Read the text again. Copy and complete the chart.

NAME	AGE	FAVOURABLE TO NUCLEAR POWER			REASON
		YES	NO	UNSURE	

5 Work in groups. Find these words and phrases in the text.

debate
unbiased
sales talk
harmless
stems
nagged

die down
echoed
open mind
handling
issues
available

lack
dangerous
device
disposal
bothered
lingered

What do they mean? Discuss and write translations of the words.

Exchange your translations with another group. Tick the translations you agree with.

Now check your answers with your teacher or in your dictionary.

3 Vocabulary Development

Noun–adjective links

Try to guess the missing nouns and adjectives. Check your answers in your dictionary. All the words are from Units 1–6.

NOUN	ADJECTIVE
beauty	
drama	
	dangerous
	interesting
friend	
peace	
	cloudy
	athletic
fame	
health	
	free
fun	

Can you see any patterns? Check if you are right. Find other words and see if they change in the same ways.

When you write a new adjective in your vocabulary book, try to find its noun. Write it next to the adjective.

2 Skills Focus: Listening

 19 Listen to Jim Leach, a representative of the CEGB (Central Electricity Generating Board), talking to Sarah about nuclear energy. Make a list of the advantages and disadvantages they discuss.

ADVANTAGES	DISADVANTAGES

 8

WB 7

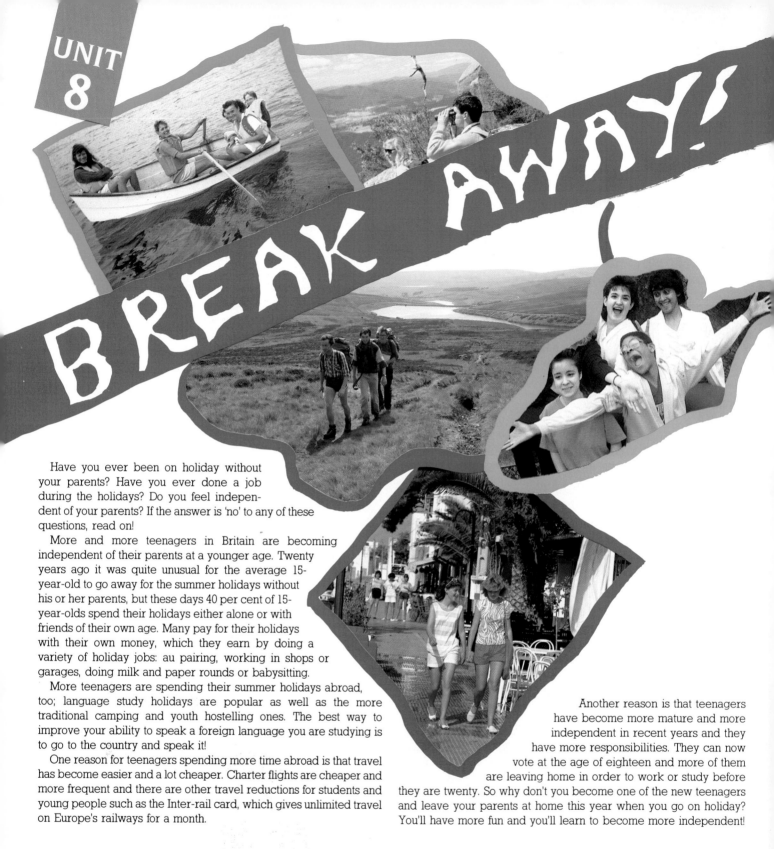

UNIT 8

BREAK AWAY!

Have you ever been on holiday without your parents? Have you ever done a job during the holidays? Do you feel independent of your parents? If the answer is 'no' to any of these questions, read on!

More and more teenagers in Britain are becoming independent of their parents at a younger age. Twenty years ago it was quite unusual for the average 15-year-old to go away for the summer holidays without his or her parents, but these days 40 per cent of 15-year-olds spend their holidays either alone or with friends of their own age. Many pay for their holidays with their own money, which they earn by doing a variety of holiday jobs: au pairing, working in shops or garages, doing milk and paper rounds or babysitting.

More teenagers are spending their summer holidays abroad, too; language study holidays are popular as well as the more traditional camping and youth hostelling ones. The best way to improve your ability to speak a foreign language you are studying is to go to the country and speak it!

One reason for teenagers spending more time abroad is that travel has become easier and a lot cheaper. Charter flights are cheaper and more frequent and there are other travel reductions for students and young people such as the Inter-rail card, which gives unlimited travel on Europe's railways for a month.

Another reason is that teenagers have become more mature and more independent in recent years and they have more responsibilities. They can now vote at the age of eighteen and more of them are leaving home in order to work or study before they are twenty. So why don't you become one of the new teenagers and leave your parents at home this year when you go on holiday? You'll have more fun and you'll learn to become more independent!

Read the article and answer the questions.

1 What are the three questions at the beginning of the article?
2 Did 15-year-olds go away without their parents twenty years ago?
3 What percentage of 15-year-olds go away alone now?
4 Do their parents pay for their holidays?
5 Why is it a good idea to go abroad if you are learning a foreign language?
6 Why is it easier for young people to travel these days?
7 When do young people often leave home nowadays?

28

1 Language Focus

BOY Have you ever been on holiday without your parents?
GIRL Yes, I have. (No, I haven't.)
BOY Where did you go?
GIRL I went to France.

BOY Have you ever had a holiday job?
GIRL Yes, I have. (No, I haven't.)
BOY What did you do?
GIRL I worked in a supermarket.

🎧 20 ▸ **Listen.**

Now practise the questions and answers in pairs. Answer according to your own experience.

SPORT	MARIA	GIOVANNI	MARCO	LUCIA
1 Have you ever played golf ?	✓	✓	✗	✗
2 Have you ever been to a cricket match ?	✓	✗	✓	✓

2 Have you ever been to Rome?

Find out about your partner's travel experiences. Make a list of ten towns or cities in your country. Ask your partner if he or she has been to them, then find out what he or she did or saw, where he or she stayed, etc.

Example

STUDENT A Have you ever been to Rome?
STUDENT B Yes, I have.
STUDENT A What did you see there?
STUDENT B I saw the Coliseum.
STUDENT A Where did you stay?
STUDENT B I stayed at the youth hostel.
STUDENT A Who did you go with?
STUDENT B I went with some friends.

3 Questionnaire

1 Write a questionnaire for your friends. Choose one of these themes.

SPORT FOOD TRAVEL MUSIC

Write ten questions. Lay out your questionnaire like the one here.

2 Try out your questionnaire on four other students. Put a tick (√) for 'Yes' and a cross (×) for 'No'.

🎧 21 ▸ **3 Four people are talking about their travel experiences. Listen and complete the chart.**

	Countries visited	Cities visited	Interesting experiences
Nick			
Jane			
Paul			
Judy			

WB 8.1–4

Who can cycle faster?

George can cycle quite well. He can cycle as fast as Wendy over a distance of 30 kilometres. George can swim further than Wendy and he can run very well. He can run faster than all the others over a distance of 10 kilometres. Alice can swim further than the others and she can run faster than Sid or Ann over a distance of 10 kilometres. Ann can't cycle very well but she can cycle faster than Alice over a distance of 30 kilometres and she can swim very well. She can swim further than Wendy, Sid and George but Ann can't run as fast as they can over a distance of 10 kilometres. Sid can cycle very well. He can cycle faster than all the others over 30 kilometres but he can't swim very well.

**Read the brain teaser and complete the chart
with the names George, Wendy, Alice, Sid and Ann.**

Name					
swim	2km	1km	5km	3km	4km
run 10km	40min.	50min.	44min.	36min.	52min.
cycle 30km	1hr	55min.	1hr 10min.	1hr	1hr 5min.

10

4 Language Focus

Sid can cycle very well. He can cycle faster than all the others.
George can cycle quite well. He can cycle as fast as Wendy.
Ann can't cycle very well but she can cycle faster than Alice.

 Listen.

Listen to some more statements. True or false?

Write three true and three false sentences about George, Wendy, Alice, Sid and Ann.

Now close your books and work in pairs.

Student A Read your sentences to your partner.
Student B Are they true or false?

Change over.

UNIT 8

5 How well can you swim?

1 How well can you do these things? Put ticks (√) under A.

	not at all		not very well		quite well		very well	
	A	B	A	B	A	B	A	B
cycle	—	—	—	—	—	—	—	—
swim	—	—	—	—	—	—	—	—
run	—	—	—	—	—	—	—	—
play basketball	—	—	—	—	—	—	—	—
ski	—	—	—	—	—	—	—	—
play tennis	—	—	—	—	—	—	—	—
play football	—	—	—	—	—	—	—	—

Now find out your partner's answers and put ticks (√) under B.

Example

STUDENT A How well can you cycle?
STUDENT B I can cycle very well.

2 Write seven sentences comparing you and your partner.

Example

I can swim better than Jo but I can't ski as well as he can.

6 Two decathletes

1 Listen and fill in the missing information about the two decathletes Daley Thompson and Jürgen Hingsen.

	Daley Thompson	Jürgen Hingsen
100m	10.44sec.	_____
110m hurdles	_____	14.29sec.
1500m	4min. 35sec.	_____
Pole vault	5.00m	_____
High jump	_____	2.12m
Long jump	_____	7.80m
Shot	15.72m	_____
Javelin	_____	60.54m
Discus	40.56m	_____
400m	_____	47.69sec.

2 Listen again. Write the verb for each event.
Now write sentences comparing the two athletes. Write four about Daley Thompson and four about Jürgen Hingsen.

Example

Daley Thompson can run 100 metres faster than Jürgen Hingsen.

WB 8.5–6

UNIT 9

MOONDOWN

Skills Focus: Reading and Listening

1 Before you read the episode, look at the first picture and answer these questions.

1 Where is Cathy?
2 Who is the man in the picture?
3 Why is Cathy in the office?
4 What are Cathy and the man talking about?

🎧 24 ▶ **Now listen and read.**

EPISODE TWO

'Now, Cathy, what's the problem? What's this letter that you want to talk to me about?'

'Here it is. You see... it's about Moondown power station. I think...'

'Just be quiet for a moment, Cathy. Give me a chance to read it, please.'

'Sorry, Mr Eastwood.'

'Mmm... very interesting. What do you want to do about it?'

'I'd like to write an article about it. I'd like to go to Moondown and ask a few questions.'

'Well, Cathy, you know very well we can't do that. How do we know this letter is genuine? It could be some madman trying to cause trouble. We can't risk it.'

'Why not?'

'Can you imagine the reaction of the director of the power station? He'd sue us for every penny we've got.'

'I suppose you're right.'

'Of course I'm right. I've been in this business a long time, Cathy. I can't take risks like that.'

'Well, why can't we publish the letter on the Readers' Letters page?'

'Mmm ... I suppose we could.'

'Oh, go on, Mr Eastwood. I'm sure the letter is genuine!'

'All right, Cathy. You can put it in the Readers' Letters section on Friday. But if there's any trouble, you're responsible!'

'Thanks, Mr Eastwood. And can I go to Moondown and ask some questions?'

'Definitely not, Cathy. We don't want any trouble with Moondown.'

'All right, Mr Eastwood. And thanks again.'

Are your answers to the questions correct? Check with your teacher.

Now continue.

Pete is waiting outside the editor's office.

'Well, Cathy, what did he say?'

'Oh, hello, Pete! Good news and bad news.'

'Right, let's have the bad news first.'

'We can't write an article about Moondown. He says it's too risky. I think he's probably right.'

'Huh! So what's the good news?'

'We can publish the letter in the Readers' Letters section.'

'Oh, big deal!'

'Come on, Pete. It's better than nothing!'

'I suppose so... Well, I'll take the letter to Jim Cathcart down in the features department.'

'OK. I'm going back to my office.'

'See you later, Cathy.'

2 True or false?

1 Mr Eastwood is the editor of the *Westfield Gazette*.
2 Cathy went to see Mr Eastwood to discuss the letter about Moondown.
3 Mr Eastwood is enthusiastic about publishing an article about Moondown.
4 Mr Eastwood is certain that the letter is genuine.
5 Mr Eastwood is afraid of the director of the power station's reaction to the letter.
6 Mr Eastwood finally gives Cathy permission to write an article about the letter.
7 He also gives her permission to go to Moondown to ask a few questions.
8 Pete is not very pleased about Mr Eastwood's reaction to Cathy's request.
9 Jim Cathcart also works for the *Westfield Gazette*.
10 Cathy and Pete work in the same office.

 3 Listen and put the sentences in order.

___ Star Point's only three miles from Westfield!

___ It says that security measures at Moondown power station are inadequate.

___ I've got something really important to tell you!

___ She says they're dumping it in the sea about 2 miles from Star Point.

___ 1.00 on a Saturday night! They really don't want people to know about it, do they?

___ Let's go and see George Parker at the town hall.

___ Go to Star Point tomorrow night, of course.

___ It also says that the people of Westfield are in terrible danger from radioactivity!

___ Mmm... I suppose you're right.

1 No, Frank. What letter?

 Listen again and check your answers.

 4 Listen once more and complete these sentences.

1 Moondown power station took about

_____

2 If Alan's in danger from Moondown, he

_____

3 Frank says they can call _____

_____

4 Cathy got a message on her answerphone from _____

5 The woman told Cathy they dump the nuclear waste about _____

_____

6 Mr Eastwood said 'No' to _____

12

_____

WB 9.1–2

Skills Focus: Writing Formal Letters (1)

1 Compare this formal letter with the informal letter in Unit 5, page 13. In what ways is it similar? In what ways is it different? Look at

the addresses
the date
the beginning of the letter
the end of the letter.

The Personnel Manager,
The Carlton Restaurant,
High Road,
Bournemouth,
BH1 3XL.

25, Smith Street,
Leeds.
April 23rd, 1987

The Personnel Manager,
The Carlton Restaurant,
High Road,
Bournemouth,
BH1 3XL.

Dear Sir,
      I saw your advertisement in the <u>Daily News</u> yesterday and I'd like to apply for the post of waiter for the summer holidays. Last summer I worked in a hotel in Bath and enjoyed it very much. I have never worked in a restaurant before but I like meeting people. I think I am a friendly, calm person and I have a good sense of humour. I can also speak a little French and Italian and think this is an advantage in a town like Bournemouth where there are a lot of French and Italian students in the summer.
      I finish school on July 18th and could start work immediately after that. I would be pleased to come for an interview any Saturday morning.
      I look forward to hearing from you soon.
            Yours faithfully,

            John Reed

      John Reed

John Smith
64 George Street
Bournemouth

16/4/89

Dear Manager,
I was reading the paper the other day and saw your advertisement. You said you wanted someone to work in your shop. I decided to write to you because I haven't got a job for the summer and want to get some money to go on holiday. We want to go to France and Germany and it's quite expensive, as you know. Also Brown's Department Store is in the same road as I live in so it's easy for me to get there. My mother says it's a good shop. I've never worked in a shop before but I'm sure it's not difficult. I'm good at Maths but perhaps that's not important any more because everyone uses calculators. I think using calculators is silly.
I can come and see you when you like, if you phone me. This is my number: 64527. We finish school on July 15th so any time after that would be great for me to start.
        Please give me the chance to show how good I am. I'm waiting to hear from you.
Yours

John

John

Notes

a When you write a formal letter you write the address of the firm on the left-hand side of the page.

b If you do not know the name of the person you are writing to, you begin the letter 'Dear Sir' or 'Dear Madam' and you end it 'Yours faithfully'.

c If you know the name of the person you are writing to, you put 'Dear Mr Smith' and end the letter 'Yours sincerely'.

d Write your signature at the end and write your name clearly underneath.

2 Read this letter. There are no grammar mistakes but it is not a good letter of application for a job. Rewrite it.

a Make the style more formal.

b Set out the letter correctly.

c Take out any information that is irrelevant.

3 Write a letter applying for a summer job. Choose from one of the advertisements below. Your letter should be set out as a formal letter. Make sure it contains the following information.

a Where you saw the advertisement.

b Your interests, personality and experience, if relevant.

c When you are available for interview.

WB 10

4/H/25

35

1 Giving directions

1 **Work in pairs. Look at the map of part of Cambridge.**

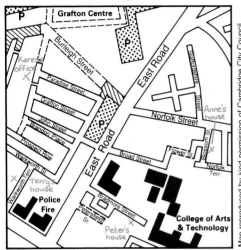

Map reproduced by kind permission of Cambridge City Council

Student A Give directions to get from the car park in East Road to one of the places listed below.

Student B Tell Student A which place it is. Give directions to get to another place.

Student A Tell Student B which place it is.

NB Try to include some landmarks in your directions.

Example
You'll see ...

the police station
Peter's house in Bradmore Street
Anne's house in Blossom Street
the car park at the Grafton Centre
Karen's office in City Road
Terry's house in Warkworth Terrace

2 **Write the directions to get to one of the places.**

2 Expressing opinions

Look at the photographs. Discuss the clothes with another student.

Example
STUDENT A What do you think of her dress?
STUDENT B I think it's awful!
STUDENT A I don't agree with you. I think it's nice.

3 What have you done?

Work in pairs.
Student A Name a verb.
Student B Use the verb to say what you've done.

Example
STUDENT A Make.
STUDENT B I've made a cake.

Student B gets a point if the answer is grammatically correct. Then change over.

Here are some verbs you can use. You can also use others.

finish   go   do   eat   drink
see   watch   play   work   have

4 Talking about experiences

Write the questions for these answers.

Example
Did you go to the concert last night?

Yes, I did. It was a very good concert.

1 _____

No, I haven't. I always go on holiday with my parents.

2 _____

No, she didn't. She stayed at home this year.

3 _____

Yes, we did. We went to France.

4 _____

Yes, I have. I worked in a shop last year.

5 _____

No, they haven't. They prefer to stay in England.

6 _____

Yes, she did. She saw the film *Stand By Me*.

7 _____

Yes, she has. She visited Paris last summer.

5 Comparing abilities

Make sentences about your family. Use this vocabulary.

speak English   type
sing   play the piano
cook   write
dance   play the guitar

Example
I can sing quite well, but my sister, Teresa, can sing better than I can.

6 Vocabulary

Here are some words that you needed to use in Units 6–10. Do you know them now? Choose ten and write sentences to show you understand their meanings.

about   funny
agree   landmark
awful   peaceful
boring   silly
dark   straight down
enough   straight on
far   well
fast

🎧 26 7 Pronunciation

Look at these words.
1 map   2 late
3 dance

Listen and repeat. Listen especially to the pronunciation of the letter *a* in each case.

Now look at these words and decide which category they belong to. Write *1*, *2* or *3*.

play ____   can ____   than ____   past ____
stay ____   have ____   bath ____   date ____
car ____   black ____ day ____   grass ____

Listen and check your answers.

GRAMMAR FOCUS

How do you do these things in English? Write a sentence for each function.

1 Give directions to get to school from your house mentioning a landmark on the way.

_____

_____

2 Give your opinion about a picture.

_____

3 Ask someone if they have been to France.

_____

4 Say how well you can play a sport.

_____

1 Directions

a **Look at these sentences.**
Go down Smith Street until you get to the pub.
Take the first on the left and it's on your right.
Go along the High Street and you'll see the bank on your right.

b **Now complete these sentences with a verb.**
_____ left at the supermarket.
_____ the second right and you _____ the bank opposite you.

c **Which form of the verb do we use when we give directions?**
Does the verb change according to the person we are speaking to?
Which verb tense do we use when giving a landmark?

2 'I think . . .'

a **Look at this exchange.**

A I think it's very interesting.
B I don't agree. I think it's a bit boring.

b **Write a sentence giving your opinion about a book you have read.**

c **It's possible to insert the word *that* in these sentences. Where?**
Is it possible to omit the equivalent of *that* in similar sentences in your language?

3 Present perfect with simple past

a **Look at this exchange.**

A Have you ever done a holiday job?

B Yes, I have.
A What did you do?
B I worked in a garage.

b **Complete these sentences.**

A _____ you ever _____ to France?

B Yes, I _____.

A When _____ you _____?

B I _____ there last August.

c **We use one of the tenses for indefinite past time, while we use the other for specific past time. Which do we use for which?**
How do you form the present perfect?

4 Irregular adverbs

a **Look at these sentences.**
I speak English very well.
She is driving fast.
He swims quite well.

b **Write two sentences about your ability to speak languages.**

c **Where do we put adverbs in English?**

37

Read the article. Underline these words.

little   much   few   many   a lot of   plenty of

£PENDING
HABITS IN BRITAIN

A survey carried out in 1987 revealed that a lot of families in Britain own a video recorder, whereas not all that long ago very few people had one. There are fashions in spending habits in the same way as there are fashions in clothes, and people are always anxious to 'keep up with the Joneses'.

What else do British people spend their money on? They don't seem to spend much money on going to the cinema and most families spend very little money on any kind of entertainment at all outside the home. They have at least one television in the house and prefer to stay at home to watch a film or a play rather than go out. They do, however, spend plenty of money on household equipment – washing machines, freezers, stereos, etc. Not many people have a swimming pool in the garden, but that is not really surprising, of course, as English weather gives very few opportunities for using one! Most families own at least one car and there are now plenty of families who have two cars.

True or false?

1 Very few English people have a video recorder.
2 English people spend a lot of money on going to the cinema.
3 English people like watching television.
4 A lot of English people have a washing machine.
5 There are a lot of houses with swimming pools in the garden.
6 It is not unusual for a family to have two cars in England.

1 Language Focus

A lot of families in Britain own a video recorder.
Very few people had one.
They don't seem to spend much money on going to the cinema.
Most families spend very little money on any kind of entertainment at all.
Not many people have a swimming pool in the garden.
There are plenty of families who have two cars.

 Listen.

Can you complete these sentences to give them the same meaning? Use these words.

many   a lot of   few   much   plenty   little

1 _____ of families in Britain own a video recorder.

2 Not _____ people had one.

3 They seem to spend very _____ money on going to the cinema.

4 Most families don't spend very _____ money on entertainment.

5 _____ people have a swimming pool in the garden.

6 There are _____ families who have two cars.

 Listen and check your answers.

2 Young people

1 Write ten sentences about young people in your country using these words.

a lot of   (a) few   (a) little
not many   not much   plenty of

These topics may help you.

school life
interests
family
possessions
ambitions

2 Read your sentences to another student. Listen to that student's sentences. Discuss any differences. Add any new information to your list.

Now write a paragraph about young people in your country.

3 Weekly eating habits

1 Read the questionnaire.

Fill in the column YOU. Find out about another student's eating habits and fill in the column YOUR PARTNER. Use these words in your answers.

a lot of   plenty of   not much   not many
a little   a few   none

Example

STUDENT A How many eggs do you eat a week?
STUDENT B None.

FOOD	YOU	YOUR PARTNER
eggs		
fruit		
sweets or chocolate		
bread		
potatoes		
hamburgers		
icecream		
rice or pasta		
cakes and biscuits		
fried food		
salads		
meat		

 2 Listen to this conversation about eating habits among British teenagers. Make notes.

3 Use your notes to write a paragraph. Begin like this:

British teenagers eat a lot of sweets and chocolates ...

WB 11.1–5

39

🎧 30 ▶ Look at the curriculum vitae.
Listen to the dialogue
and fill in the
information.

JOHN NUTTING: MOTORCYCLE JOURNALIST

CURRICULUM VITAE

NAME: _____

DATE OF BIRTH: _____

PLACE OF BIRTH: _____

SCHOOL: _____

UNIVERSITY: _____

WORK EXPERIENCE

1. _____

2. _____

3. _____

OTHER ACTIVITIES: _____

PRESENT JOB: _____

NAME OF MAGAZINE: _____ in 19 _ _

STARTING DATE: _____

_____

_____

_____

14

JOB CENTRE

JOB DESCRIPTION

An assistant is required to work in a large department store in the centre of London. The person appointed will have experience of shop work, be competent at mathematics and be able to speak at least one foreign language. In addition the applicant needs to have a pleasing personality and the ability to get on well with other people.

PERSONAL INFORMATION SHEET

NAME

ADDRESS

AGE

SCHOOL CAREER

PUBLIC EXAMINATIONS PASSED
(INCLUDE SUBJECTS AND DATES)

PREVIOUS EXPERIENCE
(INCLUDE DATES)

REASONS FOR APPLYING FOR THE JOB

ANY OTHER INFORMATION YOU CONSIDER RELEVANT

---

4 Language Focus

JOHN I've been interested in motorcycles and journalism for many years.

JOHN I've lived in London all my life.

JOHN I've been to the States and I've worked for various other magazines.

MELANIE And how long have you had this job, John?

JOHN I've worked here since 1986.

🎧 31 ▷ Listen.

🎧 32 ▷ **Paul and John are friends. Listen to Paul talking about John and complete these sentences.**

I've known John _____. I first met him

_____ when we were at school together.

I _____ in London too, then, but I don't live

there now. We both got our first bikes at about

the same time, about twenty years _____.

I think John's been interested in bikes _____

he was at nursery school! I _____ him

recently but I know _____ his present job

_____ a couple of years.

5 The interview

Work in groups of three. Look at the job description and the application form.

Student A Decide what questions you are going to ask. Then interview the two candidates.

Students B Complete the information on the form. Answer
and C Student A's questions.

6 What would you like to be?

1 It is the year 2020. Imagine yourself as you would like to be. Make notes about

your family situation (home life)
your career (what you are doing, when you started, any changes)
where you live (how long you have lived there, where you lived before)
your possessions.

2 Work in pairs.

Imagine that you have not seen your partner since you left school. Ask and answer questions about your lives. Make notes about your partner.

3 Use your notes to write a paragraph about your partner.

WB 11.6–7

Film fighters: Sir Richard Attenborough and star Kevin Kline, who plays Donald Woods

Angry lesson on freedom

by Nick Vandome

SIR Richard Attenborough's mild, grandfatherly manner belies his words aimed at the " disgusting and totally unacceptable " regime of apartheid in South Africa.

Unlike many who just condemn apartheid, Sir Richard has seen it for himself, when he visited South Africa to work on his latest film, Cry Freedom. It is the story of an unlikely friendship between the black activist Steve Biko and a white, liberal newspaper editor, Donald Woods.

Sir Richard was shattered by what he saw: " The blacks were herded into huge camps which were surrounded by imposing towers with spotlights — little different from the German concentration camps. It was an attempt to remove all human dignity but the people in the camps were still remarkably noble and courageous."

The centre point of Cry Freedom is Steve Biko's death at the hands of the authorities. Sir Richard sees this as being at the heart of the apartheid problem : " His death was more disgusting than mere physical violence. The truth is that people have legislated that this is the law."

While he was visiting South Africa Sir Richard found himself the target of white prejudice (telling the truth about the country is not looked upon favourably by the whites). He was branded a communist and a fund-raiser for the African National Congress. He was hassled by Afrikaners and eventually chaperoned out of the country by four menacing black cars. Understandably, he has little time for the police there: "Some of them are just thugs: total, total shits."

But his involvement with South Africa does not stop once he shouts " Cut" and the cameras stop rolling. The recent premières of Cry Freedom have been to help raise funds for the Waterford Kamhulaba School of South Africa, of which he is the chairman.

The school, in Swaziland, is multi-racial: there are 400 pupils from 64 different countries. Forty per cent are South African blacks and they are educated to the same standard as in any other school in South Africa.

The pupils' ages range from 11 to 17 and the aim is for them to be able to attend universities all over the world. Already the children of Desmond Tutu, and Nelson and Winnie Mandela, have been educated there — an opportunity they would not have got in South Africa.

Sir Richard hopes that efforts at places such as the Waterford Kamhulaba School will help show people that we are all members of the same universal school. Considering the recent What Next? report which suggests that British youngsters are becoming increasingly racist, perhaps it is a lesson we could all learn.

1 Skills Focus: Reading

1 Look at the photograph and the title of the article. Which of the men is Sir Richard Attenborough? Have you heard of him? What's his job, do you think? What do you think the new film is about?

2 What is apartheid? Where is it practised? How do you feel about apartheid?

3 Make a list of things you expect to find in an article about a new film. Read the article and make notes under the headings on your list. Did you find what you expected to find?

From the Guardian, 6 January 1988

4 In which paragraph do you find this information? Write *1, 2, 3,* **etc.**

____ South African attitudes to Sir Richard during his visit.

____ The names of some famous people's children who have attended the Waterford Kamhulaba School.

____ A description of the apartheid camps.

____ A comment on racism amongst young British people.

____ Sir Richard's comment on Steve Biko's death.

____ Sir Richard's connection with the Waterford Kamhulaba School.

____ Sir Richard's opinion of the South African regime.

____ An introduction to the characters of *Cry Freedom.*

____ A description of the different races which attend the Waterford Kamhulaba School.

5 Work in groups. Translate four words with your group. Pass your translations to another group. Look at that group's translations of its words. Modify them if necessary. Pass the translations on and look at the next group's list. Continue until you have seen and corrected the translations of all the words.

Group 1
belies   unlikely   shattered   herded

Group 2
imposing   spotlights   law   target

Group 3
branded   fund-raiser   hassled
chaperoned

 Group 4
thugs   involvement   chairman   aim

2 Skills Focus: Listening

🎧 33 **Sir Richard Attenborough visited South Africa before he started work on the film *Cry Freedom.* He saw many examples of apartheid while he was there. In this interview he mentions all the things in the list below. Listen and put them in order. Write** *1, 2, 3,* **etc.**

____ apartheid in public parks

____ living conditions for black people

____ curfew

____ the division of black families

____ educational opportunities

____ voting rights

____ apartheid on the beach

____ health facilities

____ career opportunities for black people

____ freedom of movement

🔺 **Listen again and make more detailed notes about these aspects of apartheid.**

3 Vocabulary Development

Prefixes

We can change the meaning of an adjective by putting a prefix in front of it. Add the prefix *un—, in—* **or** *im—* **to these adjectives and put them in the correct column. Check in your dictionary to see if you put** *un—* **or** *in—.* **You put** *im—* **in front of most adjectives beginning with** *m* **or** *p.*

tidy	dependent	safe	exciting	mature
happy	precise	adequate	polite	patient
friendly	expensive	interesting	competent	
realistic	possible	human	perfect	

Can you think of more to add to the list?

Have a page in your vocabulary books for prefixes. Give them columns, as here. Add new prefixes. When you meet a new adjective, check in your dictionary to see if you can use a prefix with it. Put it in the right column.

WB 12.1–3

WAR ON WANT

Even war won't stop us getting help to famine victims.

Over five million people in Ethiopia and Eritrea are caught up in a devastating tragedy.

They are facing starvation because of the recent drought and failure of the crops.

Yet many of them are cut off from food aid because of the vicious war which still rages.

Large areas of the country are outside Government control. And food sent through Government channels just isn't reaching them.

That is why War on Want is concentrating on alternative means of helping famine victims.

We're helping two local organisations – the Eritrean Relief Association and the Relief Society of Tigray – to get food through. And already it's working.

Because they are non-government organisations, widely supported by the local people, they can reach the stricken areas.

Now they badly need money – for food, and for transport to deliver it in time.

And they need it now if thousands of women, men and children are not to die.

Please send as much as you can. With your help today we can save many lives. Send your gift to: War on Want, Ethiopian Emergency, Freepost, Room 17D, 37-39 Great Guildford Street, London SE1 0YU.

Here is my gift. Please use it NOW to get aid to famine victims in Ethiopia and Eritrea. I enclose:

£250 ☐   £100 ☐   £50 ☐   £25 ☐   £20 ☐   £10 ☐   Other £_____

I wish to donate via Visa/Access/American Express/Diners's Club No:

Name_____

Address_____   Postcode_____

_____

Make cheques/postal orders payable to War on Want Ethiopian Emergency.

To make an instant donation by credit card please ring 01-620 1111 now.

Return to: War on Want, Ethiopian Emergency, Freepost, Room 17D, 37-39 Great Guildford Street, London SE1 0YU.

Registered charity no. 208724

WAR ON WANT   **IN THE FRONT LINE AGAINST FAMINE**

Answer the questions.

1 What country is the advertisement about?
2 What is the devastating tragedy there?
3 What are the two organisations doing?

4 They need money for two specific purposes. What are they?
5 What is the address of the organisation?

Now listen. True or false?

1 The teenagers saw the advertisement in the street.
2 They haven't got any money.
3 The things you sell at a Bring and Buy sale must be new.
4 They will send the things to Ethiopia.
5 They are going to have the sale in the church hall.

 6 Tom's house is nearer the church than Mike's.

1 Language Focus

TOM   Shall I ask Mr Jones?
MIKE No, it's all right. I'll ask him.

JANE Shall I make the posters?
TOM   Yes, that's a good idea.

MIKE Shall I keep the things at my house?
TOM   No, I'll keep them at my house.

 Listen.

Now look at these offers. Write a suitable answer.

1 Shall I buy the bread?
No, _____

2 Shall I ask John?
No, _____

3 Shall I open the window?
No, _____

4 Shall I bring some cassettes?
Yes, _____

5 Shall I invite Mary?
Yes, _____

 Listen and check your answers.

2 Making offers

Student A Read a phrase from column A.
Student B Read a reply from column B. Sometimes more than one is suitable.

A	B
Shall I open the window?	No, he's coming later.
Shall I phone Peter?	No, there's some in the kitchen.
Shall I write to Sarah?	Yes, the train is due in twenty minutes.
Shall I buy some sugar?	No, it's quite cold in here.
Shall I get your books?	No, I'll do it later.
Shall I tidy the bedroom?	No, I'll put it on.
Shall I go to the station?	No, I wrote to her last week.
Shall I order the drinks?	Yes, please. I'm really thirsty.
Shall I put on a cassette?	No, I'll get them.
Shall I do the washing up?	Yes, please. It's very untidy.

When you have finished, change roles.

Now close your books and invent similar exchanges.

3 The school trip

1 Work in groups of three.

Decide where you want to go and for how long. You need to do these things.

1 Go to the bus company to find out about a coach (availability, cost, etc.)
2 Find out about accommodation in the area (prices, facilities, etc.)
3 Find out about places of interest in the area.

Discuss what you will be responsible for.

Example

STUDENT A Shall I go to the bus company?
STUDENT B No, I'll do that because it's near my house.
STUDENT C But my uncle works for the company so . . .

2 Write a description of what you have decided to do, to give to your teacher.

WB 13.1

THE GOOD LANGUAGE STUDENT

Tick (√) the statements you think are true of a good language student.

____ You should spend some time in England.

____ You must learn at least three languages at the same time.

____ You shouldn't read English books.

____ You don't have to have perfect pronunciation.

____ You mustn't listen to English pop songs.

____ You needn't do much homework.

____ You must learn twenty words a day.

____ You should try to use the new expressions you learn.

____ You mustn't speak your own language during lessons.

____ You don't have to use a language laboratory.

____ You have to be uninhibited.

____ You needn't know about the English way of life.

When you have finished, check your answers with another student. Do you agree?

4 Language Focus

Complete these sentences.

1 You _____ go to your English lessons regularly.

2 You _____ translate everything into your language.

3 You _____ ask your teacher to help you if you don't understand.

4 You _____ be afraid of making mistakes.

5 You _____ try to revise something before each lesson.

6 You _____ do examinations to learn a language well.

7 You _____ understand every word when you read a foreign language.

8 You _____ try to speak as much as possible.

 37 ▶ **Now listen and check your answers. Sometimes more than one answer is suitable.**

5 Maths and history students

Use these words.

must   shouldn't   don't have to

should   mustn't   have to   needn't

1 Make notes about the good maths and history student.

The good Maths Student	The good History Student

2 Discuss your notes with another student. Add any new ideas to your list.

3 Write a paragraph about either the good maths student or the good history student.

6 Job applications

1 What should you do when applying for a job? Think about these points and any others you consider important.

How to write a letter of application (layout, etc.).
How to write a curriculum vitae.
What information to include in your letter and curriculum vitae (school career, hobbies, etc.).
What clothes to wear at an interview.
How to behave at an interview.

Use these verbs and write two sentences for each point.

should   must   needn't   have to

mustn't   don't have to   shouldn't

Example

You don't have to type the letter but you should . . .

2 Compare sentences with other students. Discuss any differences of opinion.

3 Listen to these two people talking about the things they think are important when they are interviewing young people for a job. Make notes.

4 Use your sentences from 1 and your notes from 3 to write a paragraph about job applications.

WB 13.2–4

MOONDOWN

Skills Focus: Reading and Listening

1 Before you read, discuss these questions.

1 What happened at the end of the last episode?
2 Where did Cathy and Pete decide to go?
3 What do you think is going to happen in this episode?

🎧 39 ▷ **Now listen and read.**

EPISODE THREE

It's half past twelve on Saturday night. Cathy is waiting for Pete in the market square in Westfield.

'Where is he? It's half past twelve and we've got to be there at one o'clock. Oh, here he comes. Hey, Pete, where have you been? I've been waiting here for half an hour!'

'Sorry, Cathy. I had to wait until my mother went to bed. You know how she worries about me. I couldn't tell her where I was going.'

'Oh, Pete ... you and that mother of yours!'

'Yes, she's become so dependent on me since my father died. Never mind ... let's get going.'

'OK. What have you got in that bag?'

'I've got two cameras, two pairs of binoculars, a cassette recorder, a torch, a radio ...'

'Oh, Pete ... we're not going on holiday, you know!'

'I suppose you're right, Cathy. But I must take the cameras. If they *are* dumping the waste tonight, I want some photographs.'

'OK, Pete, put them in the car ... and put the torch in too.'

Half an hour later Pete and Cathy arrive at Star Point.

48

'Here we are. Where shall we park the car?'

'Over there, behind those trees, Cathy.'

'It's very dark here and there's no sign of any lorries, is there?'

'No ... Let's go down to the harbour.'

'Oh, look, Cathy! The sea's really beautiful with the moon shining on it, isn't it? I've never ...'

'Ssshhh! There are some men over there! Let's get down behind this wall.'

'I wonder what they're doing. Hey, listen! I can hear some lorries coming!'

'Yes, so can I. Yes! There they are. Where are they going?'

'There's a boat over there on the other side of the harbour ... they're going over there!'

'Look at those yellow containers on the lorries, Pete! They've got that radioactivity warning sign on them! Get your camera out, I want a photo of this.'

'You see, Cathy! I told you my camera would be useful. I ...'

'Oh, shut up, Pete, and take the photos!'

'Right ... Got it. Oh no! One of the men is coming over here ... he's seen us!'

'Come on, run, Pete, run!'

2 True or false?

1 Cathy is talking to a friend at the beginning of the episode.
2 Pete is late.
3 Pete lives with his mother.
4 Pete told his mother he was meeting Cathy.
5 Pete's father is dead.
6 Pete has a lot of equipment with him.
 7 Cathy and Pete are going on holiday.

3 Put these sentences in order. Write *1, 2, 3,* etc.

____ The lorries arrived.
____ A man saw Cathy and Pete.
____ Cathy and Pete went to the harbour.
____ Cathy and Pete ran away.
____ Cathy and Pete arrived at Star Point.
____ Pete took some photos.
19 ____ Cathy and Pete hid behind a wall.

4 Read these summaries of the second part of the episode.

● The man called two of his friends and they chased Cathy and Pete. They caught Pete and asked what he was doing there. He said he wanted to take photos in the moonlight but they didn't believe him. He had to give them the film from his camera. Then they let him go and he went to look for Cathy. He was angry with her.

● As they were running away Pete fell and the man caught him. He recognised Pete because he was an old friend of Pete's father. The man asked Pete to explain why he was at Star Point at that time of night, so Pete told him that he was out for a walk with his friend. The man didn't believe him and Pete had to give him the film from his camera. The man let Pete go and he found Cathy and they went back to Westfield.

● Pete and Cathy ran away but Pete's bags were heavy and he fell. The man caught him. He was Jack Sims, an old friend of Pete's father. He asked Pete why he was there so late at night and fortunately he believed Pete's story. Pete asked him what the lorries were there for but the man told Pete to forget about them. Pete left the man and went to look for Cathy but he couldn't find her.

WB 14.1–2

20   **Now listen and tick (✓) the correct summary.**

Skills Focus: Writing
Narrating

These things are important when you are writing a story.

1 A strong beginning and ending.

Look for something surprising or unusual to say. This will make people want to go on reading your story.

2 Choice of vocabulary.

Do not always use the same words – use a dictionary to find synonyms. Look at these words and phrases. Find a synonym for each in the text.

twelve o'clock at night   trying very hard
fallen asleep   'Be quiet.'
in my direction   closer
speaking very quietly

Check your answers with another student, then with your teacher.

3 Varied sentence length.

Look at the text. You can see that the long first sentence is contrasted with the short second sentence.

4 Linking words.

These are also important. Read the text and underline all the linking words. Here are some more.

first   after that   then   finally   before   because

5 Read the text again and answer these questions.

1 There are two men in this part of the story. Which one is Harry?
2 What's the name of the man who arrives at the bungalow?
3 Where in the house is Harry's bedroom?
4 What is the first thing that makes the man think Harry is awake?
5 Why do you think Harry tells the man to take his shoes off?
6 Do you think Harry is sick or afraid? Give reasons for your opinion.

6 Work in groups. What do you think happens next in the story? What does Harry want to say to Timber? Here are some sentences from the rest of the story. They may help you to guess what happens.

'For God's sake don't touch the bed!'
Who do you think says this?

'It's on my stomach. Lying there asleep.'
What do you think 'it' is?

I went out of the room . . . and fetched a small, sharp knife from the kitchen.
Who is 'I'? Why do you think he wants a knife?

'Why don't you get a doctor?'
Who says this?

'We must administer an anaesthetic to the creature where it lies.'
A new character says this. What do you think his profession is?

'We could use ether . . . chloroform . . .'
What do these things do?

His face was white and wet.
Whose face?

'We'll give it fifteen minutes. Just to be safe.'
What is likely to happen after fifteen minutes?

'We will each take one side of the sheet and draw it back together, but very slowly, please, and very quietly.'
Why do they need to do this?

7 Here are some adjectives which Roald Dahl uses in the rest of Poison.

tense	still	warm
deadly	careful	bare
limp	nervous	safe
wet	steady	cold-blooded
sickening	angry	intense
oppressive	awful	exciting

Do you understand them? Look them up in a dictionary if you do not. They should help you to work out what happens.

8 In groups, write your version of the story. When you have finished, ask your teacher to tell you how Roald Dahl finishes it. You could also read the original yourself!

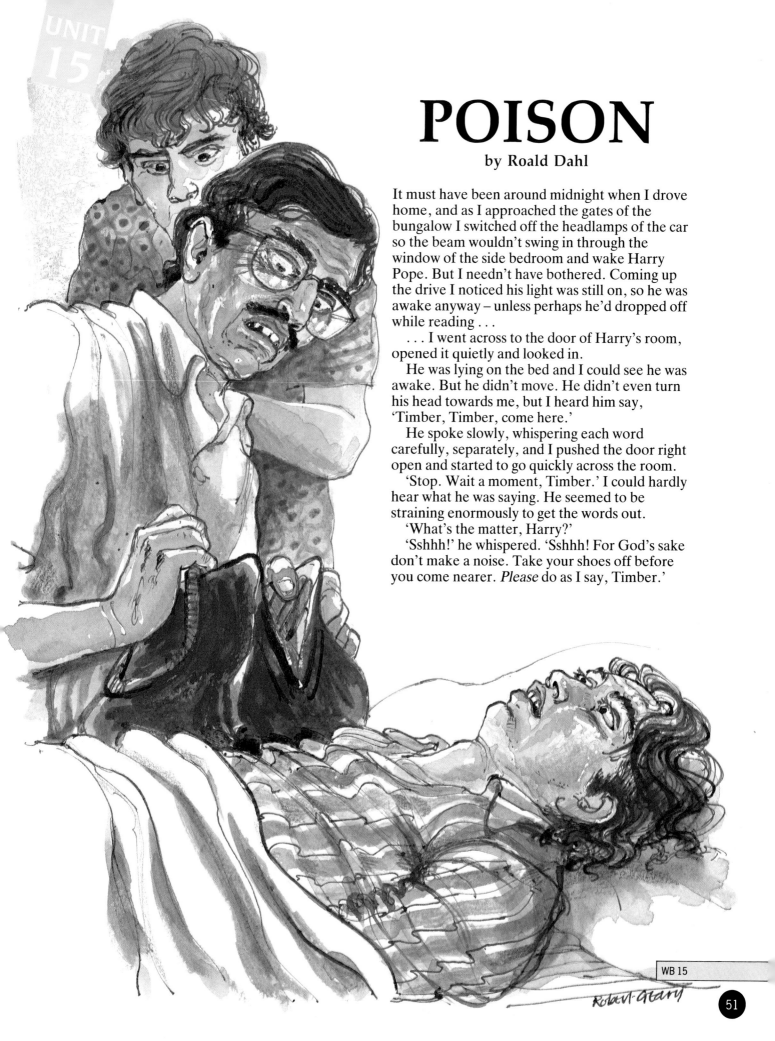

POISON

by Roald Dahl

It must have been around midnight when I drove home, and as I approached the gates of the bungalow I switched off the headlamps of the car so the beam wouldn't swing in through the window of the side bedroom and wake Harry Pope. But I needn't have bothered. Coming up the drive I noticed his light was still on, so he was awake anyway – unless perhaps he'd dropped off while reading . . .

. . . I went across to the door of Harry's room, opened it quietly and looked in.

He was lying on the bed and I could see he was awake. But he didn't move. He didn't even turn his head towards me, but I heard him say, 'Timber, Timber, come here.'

He spoke slowly, whispering each word carefully, separately, and I pushed the door right open and started to go quickly across the room.

'Stop. Wait a moment, Timber.' I could hardly hear what he was saying. He seemed to be straining enormously to get the words out.

'What's the matter, Harry?'

'Sshhh!' he whispered. 'Sshhh! For God's sake don't make a noise. Take your shoes off before you come nearer. *Please* do as I say, Timber.'

WB 15

51

REVISION FOCUS

1 Talking about quantity

Rewrite these sentences without changing the meaning. Change the words underlined.

Example

There aren't many mountains in Britain.
There are only a few mountains in Britain.

1 Few people in Britain go to church regularly.

2 There are two or three people in the room.

3 There are plenty of eggs in the fridge.

4 There isn't much milk in the bottle.

5 I've only got a little free time today.

6 We don't have many history lessons a week.

7 A lot of people are studying English.

8 She didn't eat very much food yesterday.

2 Talking about personal experiences

Put the verbs into the correct tense – present perfect or simple past.

Example

I (live) in England when I was a child.
I lived in England when I was a child.

1 I (see) that film twice and I don't want to see it again.

2 I (study) French for two years when I was at school.

3 I (be) in Paris for two weeks. I'm going home tomorrow.

4 I (live) in Italy for ten years. I like it here

5 I (be) here since half past six but he hasn't arrived.

6 I (play) tennis last week but I don't want to play this week.

3 Making offers

Write suitable offers for these replies.

Example

Shall I buy some more marmalade?

No, thanks. There's some in the cupboard.

1 _____

Yes, please. I'm really hungry.

2 _____

No, I phoned her yesterday.

3 _____

No, thanks. I've already got the tickets.

4 _____

Yes, please. It's very warm in here.

5 _____

Yes, please. I hate washing up.

6 _____

Yes, please. You make very good ones.

7 _____

No, I saw that film last week.

4 Obligation

Read this paragraph and put in the modals you think are most suitable.

YOUNG CHILDREN

Young children _____ go to bed early as they need a lot of sleep. They _____ go to school regularly but at least they _____ to go to work! They _____ watch television all the time although there are some very good programmes which they _____ watch. They _____ get up early on Saturdays and Sundays. They _____ help their parents in the house and certainly _____ keep their rooms tidy!

5 Vocabulary

Here are some words that you needed to use in Units 11–15. Do you know them now? Choose ten and write sentences to show you understand their meanings.

fashions	starvation	freezer
video	devastating	ago
recorder	harbour	war
survey	warning	gifts
since	washing	sale
journalism	machine	dumping
entertainment		

🎧 41 **6 Pronunciation**

Look at these words.

1 lunch   2 music   3 blue
4 church

Listen and repeat. Listen especially to the pronunciation of the letter _u_ in each case.

Now look at these words and decide which category they belong to. Write _1, 2, 3_ or _4._

much _____   surname _____
fruit _____   butter _____

supermarket _____   hundred _____
Thursday _____   excuse _____
bus _____   Tuesday _____
June _____   nurse _____
computer _____   true _____
burn _____

Listen and check your answers.

GRAMMAR FOCUS

How do you do these things in English? Write a sentence for each function.

1 Talk about quantities of eggs and fruit.

_____

2 Tell someone how long you have lived in your house.

_____

3 Offer to open the window.

_____

4 Tell someone about your obligation to go to school.

_____

1 Qualifiers

a Look at these sentences.

There are a lot of eggs in the fridge.
There is a lot of sugar in the cupboard.

My garden doesn't get much sun.
I haven't got many English books.

Very few English people speak Italian.
There is very little traffic on the roads today.

b Complete these sentences.

There aren't _____ people in England who go to university.

People don't spend _____ money on entertainment in England.

There are _____ of people in England who have a television set.

People spend _____ of time watching television.

Very _____ English people have a swimming pool in the garden.

We've got very _____ free time this week.

c Some forms change depending on whether the subject is countable or uncountable. Which change and which remain the same?

2 Present perfect with _for_ and _since_

a Look at these sentences.

I live in London Road.
I have lived here for five years.
I have lived here since 19__.
I came here five years ago.

b Now complete these sentences.

I _____ in the classroom.

I came in five minutes _____.

I _____ in the classroom _____ five minutes.

I _____ in the classroom _____ ten o'clock.

c What is different about your language when you form similar sentences?

3 _shall_ for offers

a Look at this exchange.

A Shall I open the window?
B Yes, please. It's very hot in here.

b Complete these exchanges.

_____ I buy some bread?
No, thanks. I bought some this morning.

_____ I invite Mary?
Yes. It's a long time since I've seen her.

c _shall_ is a future form. Do you use the future for making offers in your language?

4 Modal verbs for obligation

a Look at these sentences.

You must get up.
You should get up.
You mustn't get up.
You needn't get up.

b Match these explanations with the sentences above.

It's Saturday.
You're very ill.
It's a lovely day.
You're late.

**c Do these modals change according to the person speaking?
What are the equivalents in your language?**

53

GUIDE TO THE GALAXY

Before you read, discuss these questions.

1 What can you see in these photographs?
2 Have you ever seen one?
3 Is the object in the second photograph the
   same as in the first?
4 Can you compare the two photographs?

HALLEY'S COMET

For more than two thousand years the return of Halley's Comet every 76 years or so has been observed and recorded on Earth. Its 1986 visit, however, was the first time that humans took a close look at its nucleus. One spacecraft went within a few hundred kilometres of the nucleus. Two Soviet craft, Vega 1 and Vega 2, came within 10,000 km (6,200 miles) of the nucleus on March 6 and March 9; and most spectacularly, the European Space Agency's Giotto space probe passed within 600 km (372 miles) of Halley on March 14. Pioneer Venus Orbiter found that the cloud of gases and dust which make up the tail spread over a region about 20,000,000 km across, 15 times larger than the Sun. Scientists also discovered that the comet was losing about ten metres of material from its surface every orbit, suggesting a lifetime of about only 1,000 orbits – less than 100,000 years.

True or false?

1 Halley's Comet was first seen more than
  2,000 years ago.
2 In 1986 a spacecraft got to about 100
  kilometres from its surface.
3 Two of the 1986 spacecraft were from
  Russia.
4 The Sun measures 20,000,000 km across.
5 The comet will disappear in 1,000 years.

21

1 Language Focus

Vega 1 and Vega 2 came within 10,000 km (6,200 miles) of the nucleus.
The Giotto space probe passed within 600 km (372 miles) of Halley.
The cloud of gases and dust which make up the tail spread over a region about 20,000,000 km across.

🎧 42 **Listen.**

Work in pairs. Read these numbers.

564   5,967   8,000   25,000   123
340,520   9,000,000   7,820,645

🎧 43 **Now listen and check your reading.**

1986 was also important because of another space probe. Read the article about the planet Uranus.

THE PLANET URANUS

William Herschel discovered Uranus in 1781 but little was known about it until January 24, 1986, when the Voyager 2 spacecraft passed within

_____ kilometres of its surface. They found out that the rotation period of the planet was 17.2 hours and the atmosphere contained

_____ hydrogen and

_____ helium. The atmosphere rotates in the same direction as the planet with

winds of about _____ km/hr (_____ mph).
Before the arrival of Voyager there were five known satellites of Uranus ranging from

about _____ to

_____ kilometres in diameter. Voyager found ten more satellites with diameters

of _____ to _____ kilometres.

🎧 44 **Now listen and complete the information.**

2 Area and population

Work in pairs.

Look at the United Kingdom area and population chart.

United Kingdom, Area and Population				
	area		population	
	sq mi	sq km	1971 census	1981 census
Countries England	50,053	129,637	46,018,000	46,221,000
Northern Ireland	5,206	13,484	1,536,000	1,543,000
Scotland	29,799	77,179	5,229,000	5,117,000
Wales	7,969	20,640	2,731,000	2,790,000

Student A Copy the chart and the area data into your exercise book.
Student B Copy the chart and the population data into your exercise book.
Student A Read the information you have to Student B.
Student B Write the information you hear onto your chart.

When you have finished, change over.

Check your answers together and then in your books.

3 Geography quiz

Work in teams.

Agree on geographical areas with the other team. Write five questions with *How many...?* and five questions with *How far...?*. Give three possible answers to each question. One of these must be the correct answer.

Example
How many people live in London?
a 6,767,500
b 5,550,000
c 8,372,500

How far is London from Cairo?
a 4200 km
b 3528 km
c 2988 km

Now
Team A Read your questions.
Team B Answer the questions.

Change over when you have finished.

WB 16.1–5

I used to live in Italy

🎧 45 ▶ **Listen.**

MUM Have you finished your homework, Jane?

JANE Not yet, Mum. Oh, it's terrible. I've been here for four hours and I still haven't finished. Did you use to have a lot of homework when you were at school?

MUM Yes. I had more than you, you know.

JANE More!

MUM *And* I had to do it in a foreign language.

JANE Oh, yes. You used to live in Italy, didn't you? Was it difficult doing all your lessons in Italian?

MUM No, the most difficult thing was the number of subjects. You complain, and you're only studying three subjects. I used to study about sixteen when I was your age!

JANE Sixteen! Did you have time for anything else?

MUM Of course we did. We used to go to the sports centre two or three times a week. Because we didn't use to do many sports at school we had to go in the afternoon if we wanted to play tennis or football. And I also had piano lessons in the afternoon.

JANE I don't know how you did it!

MUM Just a question of organisation, you know! I mean, as we finished school at one o'clock we could either do our homework in the afternoon and then other things in the evening, or play tennis or whatever in the afternoon and do our homework in the evening. It was quite good really.

JANE I don't think I'd like going to school on Saturdays, though.

MUM If you've always done it you don't think it's strange at all.

JANE I suppose you're right. Anyway I'd better get on with it now, or I'll never finish. What time is that TV programme on?

MUM That's what I came to tell you. It starts in half an hour.

JANE Oh, my God . . .

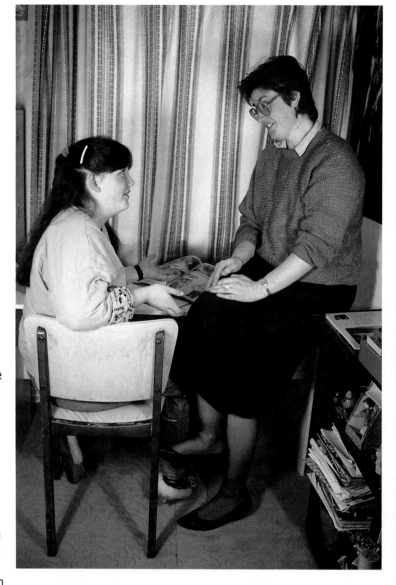

Answer the questions.

1 Where did Jane's mum use to live when she was a child?
2 How many subjects is Jane studying?
3 What, in Jane's mum's opinion, was the most difficult thing about her school?
4 Why did she use to go to the sports centre?
5 Did she like her school routine?

4 Language Focus

JANE Did you use to have a lot of homework when you were at school?

JANE You used to live in Italy, didn't you?

MUM We used to go to the sports centre two or three times a week.

MUM We didn't use to do many sports at school.

🎧 46 ▶ **Listen.**

Paola lived in England for some time. What does she say about it? Fill in the gaps in the following paragraph.

We _____ to go to school at nine o'clock but we stayed there until four o'clock in the afternoon. Of course we _____ _____ to go on Saturdays so that was a good thing. One thing I found difficult about living in England was the fact that we _____ to eat so early in the evenings! I was always hungry by about ten o'clock, and _____ to have a sandwich or something before I went to bed. I _____ _____ to drink as much tea as English people but I didn't think it was too bad.

🎧 47 ▶ **Listen and check your answers.**

5 Thirty years ago

Have things changed in the last thirty years? What did people use to do? What do they do now?

1 Complete the charts. Put a tick (√) or a cross (×).

MEN	30 YEARS AGO	NOW
Go out to work		
Cook at home		
Do the washing up		
Look after babies		
Help in the house		
Knit and sew		
Have the most important jobs		
Stay at home while their wives worked / work		
WOMEN		
Do the same work as men		
Go out to work when they had / have children		
Drive		
Look after the children		
Play football		
Do almost all the household jobs		
Do the cooking		
Have important jobs		

2 In pairs, ask and answer questions about the chart. Do you both agree?

Example

STUDENT A Did men use to go out to work thirty years ago?

STUDENT B Yes, they did.

STUDENT A And do they go out to work now?

STUDENT B Yes, they do.

3 'Thirty years ago and now.' Write a paragraph about your opinions. Begin like this:

Thirty years ago women didn't use to go out to work when they had children but now they often work and have a family . . .

6 When I was ten

1 Make notes under the chart headings. Write about what you used to do and what you didn't use to do. Compare this with what you do and don't do now.

HOME LIFE	
SCHOOL LIFE	
FREE TIME	

🎧 48 ▶ **2 Listen to two English teenagers, a boy and a girl, discussing the same topics. Make notes on what they say.**

3 In groups, compare your comments with those of other students and the two English people you heard.

WB 16.6–7

1 Skills Focus: Reading

Before you read the article, do exercises 1–3.

1 Look at the headline 'Message in a bottle'. What do you think the article is about?

2 Discuss these questions in pairs or groups.

1 Is drinking alcohol a good or a bad thing, in your opinion?
2 Do you drink alcohol regularly?
3 How much do you drink a week?
4 Do you know anyone of your age who drinks more than you?
5 Do you or any of your friends get drunk?
6 Do your parents allow you to drink at home?
7 How old were you when you first drank alcohol?
8 How much alcohol do you think it is 'safe' to drink every week?

3 Tick (√) the information that you expect to find in the article.

____ The amount of money that the British spend on alcohol every year.
____ The number of accidents caused by alcohol.
____ The age at which children begin drinking.
____ The number of young people who drink in pubs.
____ The amount of money that people under 18 spend on alcohol every year.
____ The opinions of some parents on alcohol abuse.
____ The number of young people who drink at home.
____ The names of the drinks that young people prefer.

Now read the article and see if you are right.

4 Find these adjectives in the article and underline them.

hard   staggering   cheaper   soft
brainless   legless   parental

Now complete these sentences with one of the adjectives.

1 When people have difficulty walking because they have drunk too much we can say they are _____.

2 Cocaine and heroin are _____ drugs while cannabis is a _____ drug.

3 The performance of the new Kawasaki is _____; it goes from 0 to 100 kph in 3 seconds!

4 The *Guardian* newspaper costs 30p, but the *Daily Mirror* is _____; it only costs 20p.

Message in a bottle

by Tim Madge

From the Guardian

WHILE most people probably still imagine that the biggest teenage problem is hard drugs, it is a legal drug — alcohol — which is doing the real damage.

Overall, we spend more on alcohol (£15,700 million in 1985) than we do on clothes, more than the Government spends on schools and hospitals combined. Under 18-year-olds alone probably spend in excess of £300 million a year on booze.

In 1985, 71 young people died from taking illegal drugs but a staggering 1,000 (three a day) died from alcohol poisoning. Unlike hard or soft illegal drugs, alcohol is getting relatively cheaper while more and more shops stock it.

It is of course constantly advertised — more than £200 million a year is spent advertising drink.

The facts make gloomy reading. Alcohol abuse is thought to cost up to £2,000 million a year (the government, incidentally, takes in £6,000 million in taxes on drinks).

Between eight and 14 million working days are lost to drinking; one in four admissions to hospital is attributed to alcohol abuse.

Drink is a factor in 45 per cent of road accidents involving young people and it plays a part in 50 per cent of murders and 45 per cent of violent crime.

Most worrying, the number of under-18 drinkers is rising, along with the quantities they drink. Figures are hard to come by, for obvious reasons, but a number of recent surveys have highlighted just how widespread drinking—and to excess—is among the young.

One survey found that 50 per cent of 11-year-olds drank alcohol at least once a week. A third of 15-year-old boys, and a quarter of 15-year-old girls reported drinking regularly in pubs.

By 17 (still under the legal age) over 90 per cent of boys and 35 per cent of girls were regular pub drinkers. In the past 30 years convictions for drunkenness among under 18s has rocketed by 74 per cent.

Much of this may be related to the amounts young people are now drinking. A survey of 15,000 school children by Exeter University's Health Education Unit found that nearly a quarter of 11-12 year-old children admitted to at least one unit of alcohol a week while at 15-16 over a quarter of boys and 17 per cent of girls were drinking between 7 and 20 units a week.

A unit is a half of cider, beer or lager, or a glass of wine, or one measure of spirits.

Health experts now reckon that the maximum any adult should drink a week is 14 units for a women and 21 for a man (all based on average body weights).

Over seven per cent of 15-16-year-old boys said they drank over 21 units a week. (Most commonly lager or cider).

Many drink at home—presumably with parental approval. Around a third of all the Exeter University sample (aged between 11-16) said they drank at home some time during the week before the question was asked.

Government concern about the drinking habits of the young is growing (see this week's Newsline). The message from most of those involved is that while a few drinks may be OK getting legless is brainless. And if you do get in that state you may cause a serious injury or even death to yourself or someone else.

5 Young people in Britain who want to open a bank account have to have _____ permission.

6 _____ means extremely stupid.

5 Match the numbers and the phrases.

15,700 million	The number of children interviewed in the survey.
1,000	The percentage increase in the number of arrests of under-18-year-olds for drunkenness in the last 30 years.
300 million	The percentage of boys of 17 who regularly go to a pub.
71	The safe maximum of units of alcohol a week for women.
74	The number of under-18-year-olds killed by alcohol in 1985.
90	The amount of money in pounds that the British spend on alcohol every year.
15,000	The number of deaths caused by illegal drugs in 1985.
14	The amount of money in pounds that under-18-year-olds spend on drink every year.

23

2 Skills Focus: Listening

1 Fionnoula Coulson works for the Alcohol Advisory Centre in Bath. Imagine you are going to interview her. Which questions would you ask? Put ticks (✓).

____ What is an alcoholic?
____ How do people become alcoholics?
____ How much alcohol is it safe to drink?
____ When does drinking become a problem for people?
____ How does a person's alcoholism affect the rest of his or her family?
____ Why do people drink to excess?
____ How old are the people who come to your centre?
____ What percentage of people manage to stop drinking?
____ How many people on average come to you in a year?
____ What do you do to help them?

 49 **Listen. Which questions does the interviewer ask Fionnoula?**

 24 **Listen again. Make notes of Fionnoula's answers.**

2 Compare the attitudes in your country to drinking alcohol with attitudes in Britain. In pairs, prepare a questionnaire for your class. Consider these things.

The quantity of alcohol that people in your class drink.
The age at which they started drinking.
The place where they drink (at home?, in bars?).
Their parents' attitude to alcohol.

The questions in exercise 2 of Skills Focus: Reading may help you.

Try out your questionnaire on people in your class. Compare results with other pairs.

3 Vocabulary Development

Synonyms and antonyms

A synonym is a word which has a meaning similar to that of another word. A synonym of *good* could be *nice*. An antonym has the opposite meaning. An antonym of *good* could be *bad*. In Unit 12 you looked at ways of making opposites by adding prefixes. Have you added any more to your list since that lesson?

Look at this list of words. Can you find a synonym and an antonym for them? Use your dictionary to help you. The *Collins Cobuild English Language Dictionary* often gives synonyms and antonyms with the entries. Perhaps your dictionary does, too.

	SYNONYM	ANTONYM
surface (n)		
spread (v)		
large (adj)		
finish (v)		
difficult (adj)		
cheap (adj)		
fed up (adj)		
remove (v)		
forbidden (adj)		
get on (v)		
take off (v)		
friendly (adj)		
tidy (adj)		
strange (adj)		

These words are all used in Units 16–20. Can you find more to add to the list? Keep a section of your vocabulary book for synonyms and antonyms. This will help you to acquire a richer vocabulary.

WB 17.1–3

UNIT 18

FED UP!

 50 ▶ **Listen.**

Peter is talking to his friend, Pam, after school one day.

PETER I'm fed up with school!

PAM Why? What's the matter?

PETER I've got too much homework and I have to study too many subjects.

PAM Yes, I have to do a lot of homework too. How many GCSEs are you doing?

PETER Nine!

PAM Nine?

PETER Yes – that means I have to do at least four hours' homework every night! I just haven't got enough free time ... I'm always tired.

PAM Yes, that *is* a lot. I'm only doing six.

PETER And there are too many students in my class.

PAM How many are there?

PETER There are 42!

PAM So, what's the problem?

PETER Well, I don't think we get enough individual attention.

PAM No, I suppose you don't. There are only 32 in my class. Why are there so many?

PETER There aren't enough teachers. I mean, there are over 1200 students and there are only 90 teachers.

PAM Do you do any sport?

PETER Yes, but I like tennis and there aren't enough tennis courts. There are only three. Three! For a school of this size! They haven't got enough money to build any more, or so they say.

PAM Yes, I can believe that. But what can you do about it?

PETER Nothing! Absolutely nothing! Just wait for the end of the year!

PAM Yes, things will be better at sixth form college.

PETER I hope so!

Write a sentence for each of the numbers.

Example

nine   Peter is doing nine GCSEs.

1 four _____

2 six _____

3 42 _____

4 32 _____

5 1200 _____

6 90 _____

25 7 three _____

1 Language Focus

PETER I've got too much homework and I have to study too many subjects.

PETER I haven't got enough free time.

PETER There are too many students in my class.

PETER There aren't enough teachers.

PETER I like tennis and there aren't enough tennis courts.

PETER They haven't got enough money to build any more.

 51 ▶ **Listen.**

Peter has other complaints to make about his school. Complete the sentences.

1 There aren't _____ toilets.

2 There are _____ football pitches.

3 There aren't _____ places in the library.

4 They spend _____ money on administration.

5 They don't spend _____ money on sports facilities.

52 ▶ **Listen and check your answers.**

2 Complaining

Look at the information on the chart about Peter's school.

PEOPLE		
Students	1200	
Teachers	90	
Senior teachers	6	
Secretaries	20	
Cleaners	10	

BUILDINGS		
Classrooms	30	
Science laboratories	3	
Toilets – student	8	
staff	8	
Dining hall (1)	300	places
Library	50	places
Recreation areas	4	

SPORTS FACILITIES		
Gymnasium - capacity	50	
Changing rooms	2	
Showers	10	
Football pitches	10	
Tennis courts	3	
Basketball courts	12	

EXPENDITURE PER YEAR		
Books	£5000	
Sports equipment	£1000	
Maintenance	£10,000	

Write sentences about Peter's school.

Example

There aren't enough science laboratories.
They don't spend enough money on books.

Compare sentences with another student. Have you written the same?

3 Difficult situations

1 Work in groups.

Discuss conditions in your school. Make a list of things that you're not satisfied with. When you have finished, compare lists with other groups.

Example

We study too many subjects.
We have too much homework.

🎧 53 ▶ **2 Listen to this news item about famine in Ethiopia. Choose the correct ending to these sentences.**

1 Famine is spreading from
a the south to the east.
b the north to the south and east.
c the east to the west.

2 Mr Fred Cuny works for
a the Red Cross.
b a disaster consultancy agency.
c the Ethiopian government.

3 The highlands of Harage usually produce
a corn.
b paper.
c water.

4 The lowlands are important for
a corn.
b cattle grazing.
c energy production.

5 The crops are not producing seed because
a there is no rain.
b there is no sun.
c there are not enough pesticides.

6 The number of people in Harage without food is
a 12 million.
b 12 thousand.
c 1.2 million.

7 The total number of Ethiopians hit by the famine is
a 5.8 million.
b 580 thousand.
c 58 million.

8 The amount of money needed in the countries affected by drought is
a $1.03 billion.
b $1.03 million.
c $1.3 billion.

WB 18.1–2

3 Write a short paragraph to sum up the situation in Ethiopia.

78s

78s were made of shellac and were first produced in 1888. They were played at 78 revolutions per minute (rpm) on a record player or gramophone. Sound quality was not very good. Famous musicians and singers like Louis Armstrong, Bing Crosby, Ella Fitzgerald and Buddy Holly were first recorded on 78s.

LPs

LPs (Long Playing records) were first produced by Columbia Records in the U.S.A. in 1948, and the first stereo LPs were sold in 1958. These new records were made of a plastic called vinyl and were very similar to the records sold today. Sound quality was improved but dust and scratches on the surface were still a problem. The pop industry was born as a result of the introduction of 33 rpm LPs and 45 rpm 'singles'. These records were quite cheap, so more people could buy them. The Beatles, the Rolling Stones and thousands of others recorded their first songs on LPs.

THE HISTORY OF HI-FI

Audio equipment and sound recordings are of such high quality nowadays that we sometimes forget the long evolution of hi-fi. Here is a quick guide to the history of hi-fi.

Cassettes

Tape recorders were common in the 1950s, but they were for the specialist user and were quite complicated. Compact Cassettes were introduced by Philips at the Berlin Show in 1963. They were successful because the players were small, portable and simple but music quality was not as good as that of LPs. Quality was improved in 1971 with the introduction of the Dolby noise reduction system. The record industry has suffered as a result of cassettes because a lot of people no longer buy records – they borrow them and make copies on cassettes.

Compact Discs (CDs)

Compact Discs were first produced in 1982 in the laboratories of Philips and Sony. Compact Discs are made of plastic and aluminium. They are usually recorded from digital master tapes. A laser beam is used to translate the irregularities of the surface of the disc into sound. Sound quality is excellent and they have a very long life as the disc suffers no direct mechanical contact. They are expensive, however, and recordings can't be made on them at home.

DAT

Digital Audio Tape (DAT) is a new kind of tape from Japan which is going to revolutionise home recording. With DAT, studio-quality recordings can be made (from Compact Discs, for example) on small, portable recorders. Cassettes are slightly smaller than conventional Compact Cassettes. Prices are very high at the moment but it is expected that they will be lowered when DAT becomes more popular.

Copy and complete the chart.

	DATE	ADVANTAGES	DISADVANTAGES
78s		✗	
LPs			
Cassettes			
Compact Discs			
26 ▲ DAT	Now!		

4 Language Focus

78s were made of shellac and were first produced in 1888.
LPs were first produced by Columbia Records in the U.S.A. in 1948.
Compact Cassettes were introduced by Philips at the Berlin Show in 1963.
Compact Discs are made of plastic and aluminium.
With DAT, studio-quality recordings can be made on small, portable recorders.

 Listen.

Now try to match the first and second halves of these sentences.

1	The Dolby system	are produced in Japan and Germany.
2	LPs	were developed by Philips and Sony.
3	CDs	is made in Japan.
4	CDs	was invented by Dr Ray Dolby.
5	DAT	were invented by Dr Peter Goldmark.

🎧 55 **Listen and check your answers.**

5 Compact disc production

Look at the diagram. Complete the paragraph about CD production. Use these verbs.

cut	give	produce	record
coat	develop	focus	remove
transfer	apply	press	print

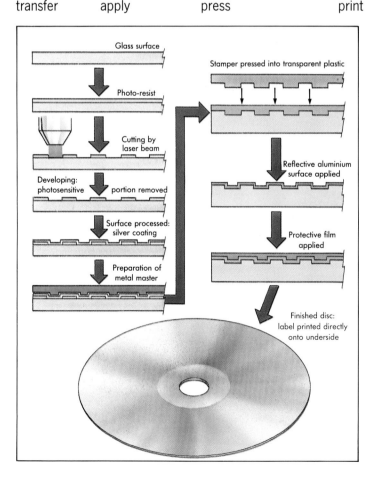

Glass surface
Photo-resist
Cutting by laser beam
Developing: photosensitive portion removed
Surface processed: silver coating
Preparation of metal master
Stamper pressed into transparent plastic
Reflective aluminium surface applied
Protective film applied
Finished disc: label printed directly onto underside

CD production is a highly technological process but it is basically quite simple. As with LP and cassette production a suitable master tape is r_____ first. This is t_____ to a new kind of master disc, made of glass. This glass disc is c_____ with light sensitive 'photo-resist'. A laser beam is f_____ on the disc and a track of 'pits' is c_____ from the disc centre outwards. (60 of these tracks would fit into one single track on a traditional LP). The disc is then d_____ and the photo-sensitive layer is r_____ chemically. The surface which remains is then g_____ a thin metal coating. A 'stamper' is p_____ from this master and then p_____ into transparent plastic to make the CD itself. A reflective aluminium surface is a_____ and then a protective plastic film. The label is p_____ directly onto the finished disc.

Now check your answers in pairs. Read your paragraph to your partner.

6 Blank cassettes and the record industry

🎧 56 **1 Michael Gilbert is talking about the effect of the sale of blank cassettes on the record industry. Listen and complete the chart with these numbers.**

36,500,000	18,500,000	25,200,000	92,598,000
81,673,000	92,500,000	56,000,000	

Sales of LPs and cassettes in the U.K.

YEAR	LPs	CASSETTES	TOTAL
1977			100,173,000
1980	67,398,000		
1983			

2 Write six sentences using the information in the chart above.

Example

In 1977 a total of 100,173,000 LPs and cassettes were sold in the United Kingdom.

WB 18.3–4

MOONDOWN

Skills Focus: Reading and Listening

 1 Listen. Which of these sentences describe what happens? Put a tick (√).

___ Cathy and Pete go to Cathy's house.
___ A police car chases them.
___ They go to Moondown power station.
___ The police arrest Cathy and Pete.
___ Cathy and Pete have an accident on the way home.
___ A car follows them.
___ Cathy manages to lose the other car.
___ They sleep in the car at Star Point.
___ Cathy and Pete go back to the harbour.
___ They follow Jack Sims to his house.

2 Before you read, work in five groups. Choose a character from this list.

the director of Moondown
Cathy
Pete
Jack Sims
Mr Eastwood

Discuss. What sort of person is he or she? In this person's position what would you do now?

 Now read on while you listen.

EPISODE FOUR

It's Monday morning at the *Westfield Gazette.*

'So you deliberately disobeyed my instructions and you went to Star Point!'

'Er ... yes, Mr Eastwood.'

'How did you find out?'

'That's none of your business, Pete!

'Mmm, it was quick work, whoever it was!'

'Shut up, Cathy! Your stupid action has caused all sorts of problems and put the *Westfield Gazette* in a very difficult position. I've spoken to the Board of Directors of the newspaper. They wanted to sack both of you immediately.'

'Sack us? For something like that?'

'I told you, it's very serious. Anyway, after a long discussion, I managed to persuade them that it would be sufficient to suspend you for a month without pay.'

'A month!'

'Yes, Cathy. And think yourself very lucky that it's only a suspension. And, of course, it goes without saying that you are absolutely forbidden to continue investigating what goes on at Moondown!'

'But, Mr Eastwood... they're dumping nuclear waste in the sea... right near Westfield!'

'They know what they're

doing, Pete! The matter is closed. I don't want to see you two for another month. Is that clear?'

'Yes, Mr Eastwood.'

'Let's go to my house, Pete.'

'OK. What are we going to do, Cathy?'

'Carry on, of course. Wait until we've got enough material and go to a national newspaper.'

'You seem very sure, Cathy. You realise what will happen if Eastwood finds out.'

'Yes, of course. We'll have to find new jobs. Let's face it though, Pete. The *Westfield Gazette* isn't exactly the *New York Times*!'

'No, you're right.'

'Here we are. Hey, the door's open! Looks like I've had visitors.'

'God, what a mess! They've half wrecked the place! Oh, and see that? Very dramatic!'

'"Keep away from Moondown! Or else …"'

'Well, at least we know one thing, Cathy!'

'What's that, Pete?'

'They've really got something to hide out at Moondown!'

3 Work in groups. Find these words in the text and underline them.

disobeyed	whoever	goes on
sack	forbidden	mess
carry on	let's face it	or else
wrecked	keep away	

What do they mean? Discuss and write a translation of the words. Exchange translations with another group. Tick the translations you agree with.

Now look at a third group's translations and compare them with yours.

Check your answers with your teacher.

4 Work in groups of four or five.

Read the episode again. Write five comprehension questions about the passage. Exchange questions with another group. Answer their questions.

 Now look at a third group's questions and answer them.

WB 19.1–3

Skills Focus: Writing Summaries

Writing a summary is difficult. It involves careful reading and accurate reporting of the important facts.

Notes

DO Read the text carefully.
Underline essential facts then make notes.
Exclude unnecessary details, examples, etc.
Write the summary as simply and clearly as possible.

DO NOT Change the main ideas of the original text.
Omit important information.
Change the emphasis of meaning.

1 Read this article from the *Observer* newspaper about an unusual holiday.

The holiday that's out of this world

by MARTIN BAILEY

A TOUR operator in London is offering the ultimate package holiday — a trip into space for £29,200 all in. Four Britons have already paid the deposit.

Twicker's World, specialists in faraway destinations, is offering 10-hour trips in a specially designed passenger spacecraft from Cape Canaveral in Florida every Thursday from 1994.

The package includes at least five earth orbits, custom-made flight suits, 'fine dining' and a view of the world as a small sphere.

The spacecraft, designed to take off and land vertically, is being developed by Maxwell Hunter II, former chief planner of the Lockheed Rocket and Space Company, and project leader of the Thor and Nike-Zeus rockets.

Yesterday Mrs Hedda Lyons, a director of Twicker's World said that the Challenger disaster had had little impact on bookings. 'Astonishingly, we have had more interest since the accident,' she said.

The Twicker's World brochure, which reassures nervous clients of the spaceship's 'exacting safety standards' states: 'You board the vehicle as you would a jet aircraft. You can either choose to remain strapped in your seat during "zero G" or get up and float about to experience weightlessness. You have your own window to view the flight and record the trip with spectacular photographs.

Seven minutes after take-off and 1,000 miles downrange from the Cape Canaveral launch site, the spacecraft goes into orbit. For the next eight or so hours, passengers will circle the earth at least five times, experiencing weightlessness.

Earthly comforts are also included in the package: 'Fine dining becomes an integral part of your experience, so you'll relish the variety of two complete meals during your voyage. A private lavatory is on board for your comfort.'

Re-entry takes an hour, with the thrusters firing for landing at 170,000 ft. Final course corrections are made and the spacecraft glides down towards the landing site. The engine re-ignites and the landing gear is extended.

The 20-passenger spacecraft is to be built by Pacific American Launch Systems of Seattle.

Twicker's World has already had four bookings for the trip, three men and a woman. Worldwide, more than 200 have paid their deposits of £2,800.

The brochure warns that passengers 'must be in average physical condition, as would be necessary for an overseas jet trip.'

2 Work in pairs. Find words in the article which mean the same as these.

a thing which has the shape of a ball
surprisingly
a sort of book which gives information, often
    about holidays
get on (an aeroplane)
a place where you sit
enjoy
journey
travel and accommodation arranged by an
    agent

Check your answers with another student, then with your teacher.

Here is a summary of the article.

Twicker's world is offering a 10-hour trip in space for £29,000 all in. Flights will leave weekly from Cape Canaveral from 1994. The spacecraft takes off and lands vertically, stays in orbit for about eight hours and circles the earth at least five times. Passengers will have two delicious meals on board, experience weightlessness and view the world as a small sphere. The 20-passenger spacecraft is to be built by Pacific American Launch Systems of Seattle.

3 Elizabeth Sutton spent her holiday in a different place. Read the article carefully.

FRIENDLY SICILY

A taste of the Mediterranean — an offer Elizabeth Sutton just couldn't refuse

Sicily is the largest island in the Mediterranean and, according to its small but passionate band of

admirers, the most beautiful. Yet every year it attracts only a fraction of the tourist hordes who converge on far smaller islands like Corfu or Majorca. Don't be put off by its image as the home of the Mafia — the people are friendly. A more down-to-earth deterrent is that a holiday in Sicily can work out more expensive than one in Greece, Spain or Portugal.

Spring comes early to the island, and the summer heat of July and August lingers well into October, which meant that the temperature was perfect for our early autumn holiday. The British Airways flight to Catania was a pleasant experience after the sardine-can suffering endured on other holiday flights to the Mediterranean. It took four hours in all to exchange the grey drizzle of Gatwick for a warm, fragrant evening in Taormina.

Taormina itself is one of the loveliest resorts in the Mediterranean, perched high on a series of lofty terraces overhanging a dramatic coastline. Accommodation here is definitely more expensive than, say, Greece, but then you're more likely to be provided with hot water and a toilet that flushes — basic facilities which Greece, for all its charm, often lacks.

There's a wide choice of places to eat, from quite sophisticated restaurants to simple snack bars. On the whole, eating out is more expensive than in many other holiday resorts — this is especially important to know if your hotel only serves breakfast. However, you do find a higher standard of service and the seafood, especially the swordfish steak, is an experience not to be missed.

A short journey by cable car takes you to the beach resort of Mazzaro, several hundred feet below Taormina. As in most Italian resorts, you pay a small sum for the use of changing cubicles, sunbeds and beach umbrella, but the beach is tidy and well-maintained and relatively uncrowded. Places of interest on the island include the capital Palermo, Syracuse with its impressive Greek and Roman remains, the fascinating Roman mosaics in the Villa del Casale and the famous Valley of Temples at Agrigento. Perhaps the most popular trip is to Mount Etna — which frequently belches out smoke to remind nervous visitors that there's plenty of life in the old volcano yet.

Find this information in the article.

1 The name of the island.
2 Two adjectives Elizabeth uses to describe the island.
3 An adjective to describe the people who live there.
4 An adjective to describe the temperature in October.
5 The food Elizabeth recommends.
6 Three adjectives to describe the beach at Mazzaro.

4 Work in groups.

Read the article again. Underline the essential information. Check what you have underlined with others in your group. Make notes. Check you have not included any unimportant details. Write your summary as simply and clearly as possible.

WB 20

REVISION FOCUS

1 Talking about statistics

🎧 59 ► **Listen to the information and complete the chart.**

TOTAL NUMBERS IN BRITAIN

	Schools	Teachers	Children/Students
Primary (5–10)			
Secondary (11–18)			
University			

Now write a paragraph using this information. Write the numbers in words.

2 Life in the past

What was it like to live in 1900? Write a paragraph about these things.

schools   work   fashion
health   family life   free time
rich and poor people

3 Complaining

Imagine you are headmaster or headmistress of your school. Write five sentences complaining about the students and staff.

Example

Too many students are late for school.
Students don't spend enough time on their homework.

4 Present passive: statements and facts

Complete these sentences.

1 Giorgio Armani clothes

_____ _____ in

Italy.

2 Japanese _____

_____ in Japan.

3 Maths _____

_____ in all schools.

4 Whisky _____

_____ in Scotland.

5 Boats _____

_____ instead of

buses in Venice.

6 Rice _____

_____ by all

Chinese people.

5 Past passive: inventions and discoveries

Who invented or discovered these things, and when?

1 radar
2 X-rays
3 colour-blindness
4 gravity
5 the electric battery
6 photography
7 chloroform
8 genetics

Write a sentence about each.

Example

1 *Radar was invented by Sir Robert Alexander Watson-Watt in 1945.*

6 Vocabulary

Here are some of the words you needed in Units 16–20. Do you know them now? Choose ten and write sentences to show you understand their meanings.

spacecraft   equipment
dust   pitches
spread   remove
lifetime   invent
surface   brochure
complain   trip
strange   seat
facilities

🎧 60 ‖ 7 Pronunciation

Look at this sentence. The most heavily stressed syllables are marked □.

Compact discs are made of plastic and aluminium.

Listen and repeat.

Now look at these sentences. Mark the main stress as above.

1 I've got too much homework and I have to study too many subjects.
2 78s were made of shellac and were first produced in 1888.
3 It's Monday morning at the *Westfield Gazette*.
4 The telephone was invented by Alexander Bell.
5 People eat too much meat and not enough vegetables.
6 Compact Cassettes were introduced by Phillips at the Berlin Show in 1963.

Listen and check your answers.

GRAMMAR FOCUS

How do you do these things in English? Write a sentence for each function.

1 Write down the number of people who live in your country.

2 Tell someone about your habits in the past.

3 Complain about the number of students in your class.

4 Say who invented the telephone.

1 Long numbers

a Look at this sentence.

There are about fifty-six million (56,000,000) people living in Britain.

b Write these numbers in words.

572

150,000

2,393,620

c What do you say between *hundred* and the rest of a number?
Do you add *s* to *hundred*, *thousand* and *million* when there is more than one of them?

2 used to

a Look at these sentences.

I used to go to primary school when I was seven.
I didn't use to go to discos.
Did you use to study English?

b Write three similar sentences.

c Can we use *used to* in the present tense?
Can we use *used to* to talk about things we did in the past and still do?

3 too much/ many, not enough

a Look at these sentences.

There are too many cars in my town.
She hasn't got enough money.
I've got too much work to do.

b Complete these sentences.

A lot of Ethiopians haven't got _____ food.

A lot of children spend _____ time watching television.

The disco was very hot and there were _____ people.

c Which of the qualifiers *too much* and *too many* do we use with countable nouns and which with uncountable nouns?
With which nouns can we use the qualifier *enough*?

4 Present and past passive

a Look at these sentences.

CDs are produced in Germany and Japan.
A lot of tea is grown in India.
X-rays were discovered by Roentgen.
The Mona Lisa was painted by Leonardo da Vinci.

b Complete these sentences.

America _____ _____ by Christopher Columbus.

LPs _____ by Dr Peter Goldmark.

Barbera wine _____ _____ in Italy.

Sony cassette recorders _____ _____ in Japan.

c Which auxiliary verb is used to form the passive?
What does the auxiliary verb agree with?
Which part of the main verb follows the auxiliary?
Is the main verb invariable in this construction?

69

YOU'VE GOT TO DO SOMETHING

Before you listen, discuss these questions.

1 Have you ever been dissatisfied with something you bought?
2 What did you do about it?
3 Did you take it back to the shop?
4 What happened?

 61 **Now listen.**

Janet is at Brown's department store.

ASSISTANT   Good afternoon. Can I help you?

JANET   Yes, I hope so. I bought these jeans here two weeks ago.

ASSISTANT   Did you?

JANET   Yes, and I must say I'm not at all happy with them.

ASSISTANT   Oh, dear. Why not?

JANET   Well, first of all they were advertised as being pre-shrunk. I've washed them once and now they're too small. They're much too small for me and they're too small for my little brother, too.

ASSISTANT   Were they washed in hot water? You know you shouldn't wash jeans in hot water.

JANET   No, they weren't. I followed the instructions on the label.

ASSISTANT   Well, that's strange. We haven't had any other complaints about these jeans.

JANET   I'm surprised to hear that. Anyway, that's not the only problem.

ASSISTANT   Really? What else is wrong then?

JANET   Well, the advertisement said they were colour fast and didn't need to be washed separately but everything that was washed with those jeans is now blue! It's too bad, you know. You've got to do something about it.

ASSISTANT   I'm sorry, dear. There isn't anything I can do.

JANET   What do you mean, there isn't anything you can do? These jeans are too small, they were expensive and they have too many things wrong with them.

ASSISTANT   I really am sorry.

JANET   It's not enough to be sorry. What are you going to do?

ASSISTANT   I'm afraid I can't do anything.

JANET   Well, do you think you could ask the manager?

ASSISTANT   I'll see if the manager is in. Could you wait a moment?

JANET   Yes, of course.

  A few minutes later.

ASSISTANT   The manager will see you now. Would you mind coming this way?

True or false?

1 Janet washed the jeans in hot water.
2 She's really pleased with them.
3 She has at least one brother.
4 The jeans were red.
5 They were expensive.
6 Janet is going to see the manager.

29

1 *Language Focus*

JANET They're much too small for me.

JANET They're too small for my little brother.

JANET It's too bad.'

 62 ▶ Listen.

Now complete these sentences.

1 I take size 5 in shoes. These are size 8.

They're _____ .

2 I take size 12 in jeans. These are size 10.

They're _____ .

3 That watch is _____ . I haven't got £80.

 63 ▶ Listen and check your answers.

JANET Do you think you could ask the manager?

ASSISTANT Could you wait a moment?

ASSISTANT Would you mind coming this way?

 64 ▶ Listen.

Now ask questions in the same way.

4 Do you think you …?   (open the window)
5 Could you …?   (do the washing up)
6 Would you mind …?   (go to the shops)

 65 ▶ Listen and check your answers.

2 *Separate the dialogues*

Can you separate the two dialogues? Write them in your exercise books.

Dialogue 1
In a record shop.
A Good afternoon.
    Can I help you?
B
A

Dialogue 2
In a shoe shop.
A Good morning.
    Do you need anything?
B
A

Good morning. Yes. Could you change these shoes, please?

Why do you want to change it?

Good afternoon. Would you mind changing this record, please?

I bought them yesterday but I think they're too small.

I had it as a present but I've got too many Madonna records. I don't want another one.

What size did you want?

No, I'm sorry, I haven't got them in grey. I've only got blue.

We don't usually change them, you know. Would you mind waiting a moment?

I need size 6. And I don't really like the colour. They're too dark.

When did you buy them?
So what colour do you want?
OK. I'll try the blue ones, please.
No, of course not.
Yes, it's OK this time. Which one do you want?
Have you got a size 6 in grey?
I'll have the latest U2 please.

Now practise the dialogues with another student.

3 Roleplay

1 Work in groups of three.

Student A **You are the customer.**
Student B **You are the shop assistant.**
Student C **You are the manager.**

Look at your information below.

CUSTOMER You bought a sweater two weeks ago. It cost £50. The label said it was machine-washable and colour fast. The shop assistant confirmed this. You washed it once, it shrank and the colours ran. It also has a lot of holes in it now. You want a new sweater or your money back. You can't find the receipt.

NB
You are very pleasant at first.
Ask the assistant politely if he or she will change it.
Remain polite unless you can't get what you want.

ASSISTANT You weren't the assistant who sold the sweater. You have one the same and have had no problems with it. The rule of the shop is that you mustn't change goods if the customer doesn't have the receipt. In extreme cases you can call the manager.

NB
Greet the customer politely.
Ask when he or she bought the sweater.
Explain you have the same sweater and have had no problems with it.
Ask for the receipt.
Explain you can't do anything.
Offer to get the manager.

MANAGER You have been manager of this shop for many years and are proud of its reputation. You are always very polite with people but think rules must be respected. You very rarely do anything for customers if they don't keep the receipt.

NB
Greet the customer politely.
Ask for the receipt.
Apologise but say you can't do anything.
Say you have been in the shop for years and always try to do your best.
Make your final decision.

66 ▶ 2 Listen to these people complaining.

1 What are they complaining about?
2 What's wrong with the things?
3 Do they get satisfaction?

WB 21.1–5

Before you read, discuss these questions.

1 Do you think Madonna was a happy child?
2 Do you think she is happy now?

MADONNA

Madonna Louise Ciccone was born on 16th August 1959 in Michigan, the state where she lived during her childhood and early adolescence. Madonna, whose mother died when she was only six years old, had a rather unhappy family life. Her father married again, creating a situation which Madonna tried in every way to change, but without success.

She gradually became very involved in her passion for contemporary dance. She won a scholarship to study dance at the University of Michigan, where she met Steve Bray, a black musician, who wrote several songs for her album *Like a Virgin*. Long after her relationship with Steve Bray had finished she remained very good friends with him.

In 1982 she made her first single, *Everybody*. It was a great success and it was this record that started her on the rapid rise to fame. Perhaps the song which has had most success so far is *Into the Groove*, which she made in 1985. Apart from singing she has also appeared in several films, of which the most successful is *Desperately Seeking Susan*.

Answer the questions.

1 Where was Madonna born?
2 What was her first interest?
3 Who was Steve Bray?
4 Name two songs that Madonna sings.
5 Name one of her films.

30

4 Language Focus

Madonna was born in Michigan, where she lived during her childhood.
Madonna, whose mother died when she was six, was unhappy when her father remarried.
Steve Bray was a black musician who wrote several songs for her.
It was the record *Everybody* which started her on the rapid rise to fame.
Madonna has also appeared in several films, of which the most successful is *Desperately Seeking Susan*.

 67 **Listen.**

Now read and complete these sentences.

Beautiful, talented and ambitious are three words _____ people use to describe Madonna.

Madonna, _____ family is very large, is the eldest of the daughters.

In 1980 she went to Paris, _____ she stayed for only a few weeks.

Shanghai Surprise, _____ she appeared with Sean Penn, was not well received by the critics.

She describes herself as a woman _____ knows what she wants and is determined to get it.

68 **Listen and check your answers.**

5 Boris Becker

Read these notes about Boris Becker and write a paragraph about him. Use as many relative clauses as you can.

Boris Becker
German
Tall, blond hair, blue eyes
Comes from Leiman, near Heidelberg
Born November 22nd 1967
Father architect – designed and built tennis centre
Learnt tennis at this centre
Played soccer before tennis

Gunther Bosch – coach – introduced him to Ion Tiriac, manager – 1985, 1986 won Wimbledon championship
Youngest person to win Grand Slam tournament
Continues to win championships

Begin your paragraph like this:

Boris Becker, who is German and ...

Check your work with another student. Work together and try to improve your paragraph. Add more information about Boris Becker if you can.

6 People, films, places

Complete these sentences.

PEOPLE

1 I like people who _____

2 I hate people whose _____

3 I get annoyed with people who _____

4 I am attracted to people whose _____

FILMS

5 I love films in which _____

6 I get bored with films which _____

7 I laugh at films which _____

8 I never go to films which _____

PLACES

9 I like towns where _____

10 I hate beaches where _____

11 I get bored in places which _____

12 I get excited about places where _____

Now work in pairs. Find out about your partner's opinions. Make notes.

Write three paragraphs about your partner. Begin like this:

Maria likes people who ... but she hates people who ...

WB 21.6–9

1 Skills Focus: Reading

1 Before you read the article, discuss these questions in groups.

1 What is acid rain?
2 What is your country doing about the problem?

2 Read the article quickly and find the paragraph in which the writer

1 explains how acid rain affects trees. _____
2 mentions the cost of air pollution to Europe. _____
3 mentions the cost of reducing sulphur emissions. _____
4 mentions the things that acid rain damages. _____
5 talks about the connection between acid rain and senile dementia. _____

Who is the 'dirty old man' in the headline?

3 Find these words in the text.

damage   health
reduce   environmentalists
soil   imbalances
sulphur   emissions
join   unprecedented

What do they mean? In groups, discuss and write translations.

Now look at the same words in these sentences.

I had to pay a lot to repair the damage done to my car in the accident.
He is never ill: he is in very good health.
The government reduced the cost of petrol from £1 per litre to 80p per litre.
Environmentalists have been protesting about the excessive use of pesticides.
Soil is the substance in which plants and trees grow.
There is an imbalance of opportunities between blacks and whites in South Africa today.
Acid rain contains the chemical sulphur, which has the chemical symbol S.
Emission is a formal word which we use to talk about the release of gas or radiation into the atmosphere.
Join means 'to become a member of'.
If something has never happened before we can say it is unprecedented.

Were your translations correct? Check with your teacher.

The Dirty Old Man of Europe

ACID RAIN causes damage to buildings, farms and fisheries, forests and lakes and to human health. The British government has done little to reduce the damage caused by acid rain in the last few years. This damage costs the European Community more than $12 billion every year. Environmentalists have discovered that Britain is responsible for the greatest amount of European air pollution, but the government has only recently decided to take any action.

When acid rain falls onto soil it absorbs the aluminium from the soil and carries it into rivers and lakes. In June 1988 a report in the *Observer* suggested a connection between senile dementia and aluminium in drinking water in many parts of England and Wales.

When it falls onto plants (including trees) it causes severe chemical imbalances, resulting in death. In 1985 a survey by the Friends of the Earth discovered that over two thirds of the trees examined had suffered from the effects of acid rain.

Britain, and especially the Central Electricity Generating Board (CEGB), is the largest single polluter of European air. The power stations around Selby produce more sulphur than Portugal, Norway, Ireland and Switzerland together. According to the Friends of the Earth more than 70 per cent of British sulphur emissions fall outside Britain.

Other European nations have seen the damage and have started to act. They have formed a club which is trying to reduce the sulphur emissions by 30 per cent by the year 1993. Britain, however, has constantly refused to join this club, even though the cost of the reduction would only be about £2 billion over ten years. If the government does not take drastic action very soon, there will be an unprecedented crisis in the European ecology in the very near future.

4 Match the numbers and dates with the sentences.

1 $12 billion — The cost of reduction in sulphur production over 10 years.

2 June 1988 — The amount of British pollution which falls on Europe.

3 1985 — The sum of money that Europe spends because of pollution every year.

4 70% — The date of a newspaper report about senile dementia.

5 30% — The date of a survey by the Friends of the Earth.

6 £2 billion — The amount by which the European club hopes to reduce pollution by 1993.

▲31

2 Skills Focus: Listening

David Job works in environmental education at the Slapton Ley Field Studies Centre in Devon. Paul asks him about the problem of acid rain.

🎧 69 **Listen and put Paul's questions in order. Write** *1, 2, 3*, **etc.**

_____ What else needs to be done urgently about this problem?

_____ What's the single most important cause of acid rain?

_____ What's the government doing about it?

_____ What is acid rain exactly?

_____ What are the main effects of acid rain in Great Britain?

Listen again. Complete the statements. Use these words.

nitrogen   trees   disease   acid   international
power stations   rivers   sulphur   North America
lakes   behind   acid rain   vegetation   little

_____ There are two main causes of concern: one is to

do with the effects on _____ and

_____, and the other is perhaps more to

do with the effects on _____.

_____ Rain is naturally _____.

_____ Well, in Britain the government is doing very

_____ at present.

_____ We have coal- and oil-fired _____, which

generate a fair amount of oxides of _____.

_____ ... the most important thing is to recognise the

_____ nature of the problem.

_____ ... we have vehicle fumes, which are

particularly rich in oxides of _____.

_____ I think we're a long way _____ other EEC

countries and _____.

_____ There are many causes, perhaps, of damage to

_____, some of which may be due to

_____, some of which may be due to

_____.

Now match the statements and questions. Write *1, 2, 3*, **etc.**

3 Vocabulary Development

Adjective–adverb link

Can you find the adverbs which come from these adjectives? You can use your dictionary to help you.

ADJECTIVE	ADVERB
obstinate	
useful	
fantastic	
fast	
good (better best)	
bad (worse worst)	
careful	
late	
separate	
terrible	
probable	
easy	
real	
formal	
hard	

Sometimes it is easy to make an adverb from an adjective. Can you form any rules for doing this?

You can form two adverbs from some adjectives in this list. Find them and write sentences to show you understand the different meanings.

Some adjectives are exactly the same as their adverbs. Which ones?

Can you think of any more to add to the list?

WB 22.1–3

75

This is an extract from a secret White House document which was declassified in January 1987. The document may or may not be genuine, however.

BODIES of four 'aliens' from a crashed UFO (unidentified flying object) were recovered and examined by a special American government team 40 years ago. A mysterious committee code-named Majestic 12 was set up to examine the aliens. On 24th June 1947 some disc-shaped craft were sighted in the United States. Little was learned about the objects until a local man reported that one had crashed in a remote region of New Mexico, about 75 miles north-west of Roswell Army Air Base.

On 7th July 1947, a secret operation was begun to recover the wreckage of this object for scientific study. During the course of this operation, it was discovered that four small human-like beings had apparently ejected from the craft some time before it exploded. They had fallen to earth about two miles east of the wreckage site.

All four were dead and badly decomposed due to predators and exposure to the elements. Approximately one week had passed before they were discovered. A preliminary consensus (19th September 1947) showed that the disc was probably a short-range reconnaissance craft...

DECLASSIFIED

Here is how some UFO experts reacted to the discovery of the document.

The document must be genuine. Majestic 12 was a committee of senior US officials which investigated and then covered up news of flying saucer crashes.

The document may be genuine but there are some things wrong with it—for example, there is no signature on it.

The document might be genuine because there is also a memo to General Twining about an 'MJ 12' briefing for President Eisenhower. But this memo might also be a forgery.

The document can't be genuine. There are no records of the existence of the Majestic 12 committee apart from this document and the memo.

But what do _you_ think? Was there a UFO crash in 1947? Is the document genuine? Did members of MJ 12 really establish the existence of UFOs?

Answer the questions.

1 When did the events described in the document take place?
2 Why was the committee Majestic 12 set up?
3 When did the UFO crash?
4 Who reported the crash?
5 How many aliens did they find?
6 Were there any survivors?
7 Where did they find the bodies of the aliens?
8 Does everyone agree that the document is genuine?

33

1 Language Focus

	Degree of certainty
The document must be genuine.	100%
The document may be genuine.	40%
The document might be genuine.	30%
The document can't be genuine.	0%

NB *may* and *might* have almost the same meaning and are often interchangeable!

🎧 70 **Listen.**

Now complete these sentences.

1 There _____ be life on the moon because there is no oxygen.

2 There _____ be life on other planets.

3 UFOs _____ exist.

4 I waited for three hours and the bus didn't come. There _____ be a bus strike.

🎧 71 **Listen and check your answers.**

2 Animal tracks

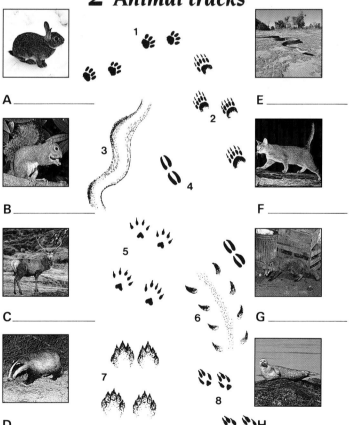

A _____

B _____

C _____

D _____

E _____

F _____

G _____

H _____

Match the animals and the tracks. Discuss your answers with another student.

Example

STUDENT A What's number one?
STUDENT B It might be a badger.
STUDENT A I don't agree. I think it must be a deer.

3 Do these things exist?

1 **Complete the chart with ticks (✓).**

	CAN'T 0%	MIGHT 30%	MAY 40%	MUST 100%
UFOs				
the Yeti				
Ghosts				
life after death				
the Bermuda Triangle				
the Loch Ness Monster				
life on other planets				

In groups, compare your answers.

Example

STUDENT A Do you believe in UFOs?
STUDENT B I don't know. They may exist.
STUDENT C Of course they don't. They can't possibly exist.
STUDENT D I disagree. They must exist. People have seen them.

🎧 72 **2 Listen to Chris and Paul discussing the same things. What do they believe in? Make notes.**

3 Use your notes to write a paragraph about the things people do and do not believe in.

WB 23.1–3

77

🎧 73 **Listen and read.**

True or false?

1 The two friends are bored.
2 They don't usually go away at the weekend.
3 They decide to go to London.
4 Bournemouth is a seaside town.
5 They decide to go by train.
6 They haven't got enough money to go away.
7 They enjoy their weekend.

4 Language Focus

GIRL If it rains, we'll go to London.
GIRL If it's sunny, we'll go to the seaside.
BOY If we go by train, it'll cost a lot of money.

🎧 74 ▶ **Listen.**

Now complete these sentences.

1 If it _____ , I _____ skiing this weekend.

2 If you _____ to my house, I _____ you my new computer.

3 If you _____ to England this summer, you _____ speak English.

🎧 75 ▶ **Listen and check your answers.**

5 Travel quiz

Complete the sentences.

Example

If you go from Dover to London by train, you will arrive at *Victoria* Station.

1 If you go to Quebec, you will hear people speak _____ .

2 If you go to Rio de Janeiro in December, the weather will be _____ .

3 If you go to the U.S.A., you will have to put your watch back _____ hours.

4 If you want to climb Mount Fuji, you will have to go to _____ .

5 If you want to see the Taj Mahal, you will have to visit _____ .

6 If you want to see the tallest building in the world, you'll have to go to _____ .

7 If you want to visit the Forbidden City, you will have to go to _____ .

8 If you want to go for a trip on the River Thames, you will have to visit _____ .

9 If you stay in Bangor, you will hear people speak _____ .

10 If you go to _____ , you will see the Golden Gate Bridge.

11 If you visit Australia at Christmas, the weather will be _____ .

12 If you want to see St Mark's Square, you will have to visit _____ .

13 If you go to _____ , you will be able to visit the Parco Gaudi.

14 If you go to Jersey, you will hear people speak _____ .

15 If you want to climb Mount Snowdon, you will have to go to _____ .

Compare answers with another student.

🎧 76 ▶ **2 Now listen to three English people doing the same exercise. Compare your answers.**

3 Write six similar sentences, three true and three false. Exchange sentences with another student. Say if his or her sentences are true or false.

6 Consequences

Work in groups. Take turns to make 'If' sentences using these words.

holiday	London	Victoria Station	Underground
hotel/Knightsbridge	dinner/8.00	bed/11.00	
get up/8.00	breakfast/8.30	sightseeing/morning	
Buckingham Palace	lunch/1.00	shopping/afternoon	
spend/money	go home		

Example

STUDENT A If you have a holiday, you'll go to London.
STUDENT B If you go to London, you'll arrive at Victoria Station.
STUDENT C If you arrive at Victoria Station, . . . **etc.**

If you can't make a sentence in ten seconds, you will be out of the game!

WB 23.4–5

79

MOONDOWN

Skills Focus: Reading and Listening

1 Before you read, discuss these questions.

1 Are Cathy and Pete going to continue with their investigation of Moondown, in your opinion?
2 What do you think they are going to do with the photographs that Pete took?

 Now listen and read.

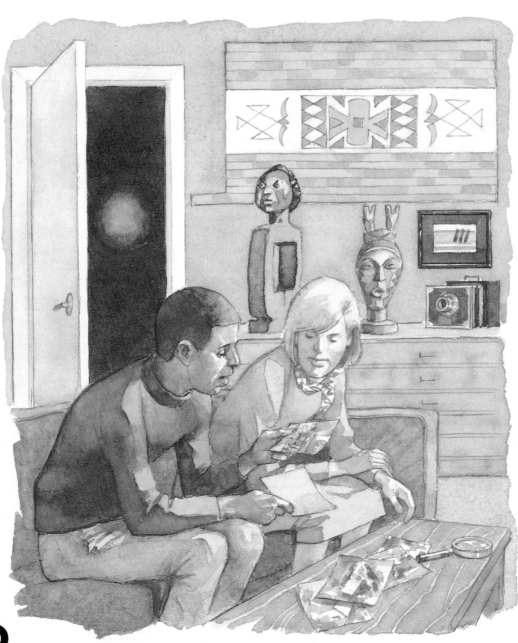

EPISODE FIVE

Cathy comes to Pete's house.

'Hi, Cathy. Come in.'

'Thanks. Well, have you got them?'

'What?'

'The photographs, of course!'

'Oh ... yes, of course. Here they are. Not bad, eh?'

'Oh, Pete, they're excellent! Very clear!'

'Yes ... and look at this one ... nice, isn't it?'

'Pete, you fool, I didn't see you take that!'

'Good, isn't it?'

'No, it isn't. Give it to me. My nose isn't like that!'

'Yes, it is. The camera never lies. Anyway, what are we going to do today?'

'I'll send these photos to the *Daily Clarion* in London. I've got a friend who works for them. I'll see what she says. Then I want to go to the director of Moondown's house. I want to see if he drives a Rover!'

'What shall I do, Cathy?'

'Go and see Jack Sims. Try to get some information from him – anything.'

'Right. Let's go. I'll see you here at one o'clock.'

'Bye.'

Pete is at Jack Sims' house.
  'Who is it?'
  'It's me, Pete Chisman, Mr Sims.'
  'What do you want?'
  'I need to talk to you, Mr Sims. Let me in.'
  'I don't want to talk to you! Go away!'
  'Oh, come on, Mr Sims. Just a few minutes. Please!'
  'Oh, all right. Come in, then. But just five minutes, mind.'
  'Thanks.'
  'You're just like your dad was. Stubborn!'
  'Mmm... I know.'
  'Now, what do you want? If it's about Moondown, I'm not saying anything.'
  'But can't you see the danger of dumping that waste in the sea, Mr Sims?'
  'Listen, Pete. Until last year I was out of a job, unemployed, and at 55 years of age that's serious. Now I've got a job driving the lorries for them. The money's good and the

work's easy, although the hours are a bit long...'
  'You said "until last year". Does that mean that you've been dumping waste there for more than a year?'
  'I'm not saying anything. You already got me into trouble the other night. The director wanted to see me personally on Monday morning. He wanted to know who I was talking to on Saturday night.'
  'Did you tell him?'
  'Of course not. Your dad and I were great friends.'
  'That's strange! Then how did the director of the power station find out that it was us?'
  'I don't know, but it wasn't me. Anyway, I'm not saying anything else. You've had your five minutes.'
  'All right, Mr Sims. And thanks.'
  'Bye now, Pete. And you be careful. I don't trust some of those people at Moondown!'

2 Look at these words and phrases. Find words in the text which mean the same.

not to tell the truth	(v)	to	_____
to leave	(v)	to	_____
obstinate	(adj)		_____
with no job	(adj)		_____
the time spent working	(n)		_____
not to take risks	(v)	to	_____

3 Answer the questions.

1 What does Cathy want to see when she gets to Pete's house?
2 Why does Cathy call Pete a fool?
3 Does Cathy like her photo?
4 What is Cathy going to do with the other photos?
5 Why does Cathy want to know if the director of Moondown drives a Rover?
6 Does Pete go with Cathy?

4 True or false?

1 Jack Sims is pleased to see Pete.
2 Pete agrees that he is like his father.
3 Jack Sims is working for Moondown because he didn't have a job for a long time.
4 Jack Sims likes his job.
5 Jack Sims started working for Moondown three years ago.
6 Jack asked to see the director of Moondown last Monday.
7 Jack told the director he had seen Pete on Saturday.
 8 Jack seems to think that Pete is in danger.

 5 Listen to the second part of the episode. Answer the questions.

1 Was Cathy there when Pete got home?
2 What did Cathy find out about the white Rover?
3 Where is Cathy?
4 Who phoned Cathy when she got home?
5 Where does Cathy arrange to meet Pete?
6 Is she there when Pete arrives?
7 Did the barman see Cathy?
8 Who left the pub with her?
9 Why is Pete worried?

Skills Focus: Writing
Reports

Wednesday about midnight.

Between Augustus Road /
Whitlock Drive.

Heard someone behind them.

Saw three boys.

Snatched woman's bag.

Daughter tried to stop them.

Pushed to ground, bag snatched.

Suspects black, late teens.

Jeans, training shoes.
One had check shirt.

Contents of bags: cheque books,
cards, money, letters.

MOTHER AND DAUGHTER ROBBED

A MOTHER and daughter were robbed by a gang of youths as they were walking through an alleyway between Augustus Road and Whitlock Drive, Wimbledon Park, just before midnight on Wednesday last week.

The two were walking through the alleyway when they heard footsteps behind them.

They turned round to look and saw three youths running towards them.

One of the youths snatched the mother's handbag from her shoulder, breaking the strap.

The daughter attempted to keep hold of her bag, but was pushed to the ground; the bag was then snatched and the three youths ran off.

The suspects are described as black, aged in their late teens, wearing jeans and training shoes and one wore a chequered shirt.

The bags contained various cheque books and cards, cash and correspondence, some of which was recovered the next day in the Clapham area and handed in to the police.

1 Look at the two texts. Which one is a report?

2 Read the report carefully. Underline any examples of the passive (_ _ _ _) and of the simple past (_____). Circle any linking words.

3 The other text consists of the notes from which the report was written. Read them. Which of the notes are linked? How are they linked?

When you are reporting actions and events these things are important.

a The language you use should be clear, simple, formal and impersonal.
b You need to be able to use the past tenses in English clearly and accurately. Passives are frequently used.
c Linking words are important, particularly time links (*after, before, then, as, when*).

4 Read these notes about a road accident.

3.15 pm Friday: accident on
A48 near Chepstow.

Car and coach involved.

Car going up hill – coach coming
down.

Road conditions: snow and ice.

Coach skidded on ice,
collided with car.

Car driver in hospital – broken leg.

Coach driver not hurt.

Pedestrian hit by car. In hospital.

Witnesses: woman walking along street.
man heard crash,
went to window.

Complete this report of the accident using the notes.

5 Read these notes.

4.45 pm Friday.
Large department store.
Man running out.
Stopped by store detective.
Searched.
Perfume and jewellery in
pockets.
Wanted to give girlfriend
surprise!
Arrested.

Write a report of this incident using the notes.
Make sure you use linking words when possible
and also the passive when necessary.

There _____ an accident _____ at 3.15 pm on the A48 _____ . A car
and a coach _____ . The car _____ up the hill _____ the coach
_____ . There _____ a lot of snow and ice on the road. The coach
_____ on the ice _____ it _____ with the car. The car driver
_____ in hospital _____ a broken leg _____ the coach driver
_____ . A pedestrian _____ by the car _____ is now in hospital. There
_____ two witnesses, one a woman who _____ along the street and the
other a man who _____ the crash and _____ to the window.

WB 25

REVISION FOCUS

1 Complaining

Look at the pictures and write sentences about them.

Example

This hat is too big.

2 Polite requests

Match the requests and the answers.

1 Do you think you could close the window, please?
2 Would you mind changing this shirt, please? It's too small.
3 Would you mind getting the manager, please?
4 Could you turn the stereo down, please?

_____ Yes, OK. I didn't realise it was so loud.
_____ No, I'm sorry. He's not here at the moment.
_____ Certainly. Have you got a receipt for it?
_____ No, I'm sorry. It's too hot in here.

Now ask and answer the questions in pairs to check if you are right.

3 Relative clauses: talking about holidays

Write sentences about your holidays.

Example

We stayed in a town on the coast where the sea sometimes covered the road.

Think about

your hotel   someone you met   a beach
transport you used   a meal you ate
a place you visited

4 Expressing certainty and uncertainty

Say where these people may/might/must/can't be at the moment.

Example

Your father.

My father must be at home now. He can't be at work at this time of day.

1 Your brother/sister.
2 A student who is absent from class today.
3 Your headmaster/headmistress.
4 Your country's president.

5 Talking about future possibilities (1)

Complete the sentences.

Example

If I pass my exams,

a *I'll leave school and work for a year.*
b *Then I'll go to university.*
c *After that I'll go to England.*

1 If I go to university,
a I'll study medicine.
b Then _____.
c After that _____.

2 If I go to England,
a I'll _____.
b _____.
c _____.

Now do the exercise again. Write alternative answers.

6 Vocabulary

These are some of the words you needed in Units 21–25. Do you know them now? Choose ten and write sentences to show you understand their meanings.

advertised	damage	sightseeing
complaint	health	show
childhood	genuine	stubborn
scholarship	exist	be careful
fame (famous)	ghost	to lie
pollution		

🎧 79 7 Pronunciation

Look at these words.

1 met   2 verb
3 departure   4 absent
5 female

Listen and repeat. Listen especially to the pronunciation of the letter *e* in each case.

Now look at these words and decide which category they belong to. Write *1, 2, 3, 4* or *5.*

fern _____   decide _____
definitely _____   sister _____
decent _____   invent _____
decompose _____   reply _____
help _____   example _____
serve _____   brother _____
she _____   afternoon _____

Listen and check your answers.

GRAMMAR FOCUS

How do you do these things in English? Write a sentence for each function.

1 Describe a pair of jeans which are size 10 when you take size 12.

_____

2 Ask someone politely to open the window.

_____

3 Make these two sentences into one.
This is the woman. She lives in Paris.

_____

4 Express uncertainty about the existence of UFOs.

_____

5 State your intentions for this weekend if the weather is fine.

_____

1 (much) too + adjective

a Look at these sentences.

These jeans are too small.
These jeans are much too small.
There are too many students in the class.
There is too much traffic in the town.

b Complete these sentences.

Those shoes are very nice but they're _____ big.

That restaurant is very good but it's much _____ expensive.

There are _____ _____ cars on the roads these days.

c *much* goes before *too* when an adjective follows.
much goes after *too* when a noun follows.

2 'Would you mind ...?'

a Look at these sentences.

Would you mind going to the shops for me?
Do you think you could go to the shops for me?
Could you go to the shops for me?

b Complete these sentences.

_____ opening the window?

_____ open the window?

Do you think _____ open the window?

c Put these sentences in order, starting with the most polite.

3 Relative clauses

a Look at these sentences.

That's my friend who speaks four languages.
The book which I'm reading is very good.
That's the place where we stayed.
He's the man whose son lives near us.

b Complete these sentences.

The book _____ is on the table is Mary's.
Mary is the girl _____ lives in New York.
She's the girl _____ father is a postman.
The place _____ I went for my holidays is very beautiful.

c What do you notice about the construction with *whose*?

4 Modal verbs

a Look at these sentences.

She's moved into a smaller house and sold her car. She must need the money.
It's cloudier than yesterday. It may rain later.
Patrick was with me at the time of the murder so he can't be guilty.
He's one of the fastest runners in the world so he might win the gold medal.

b Complete these sentences.

I saw Sue in town this morning, so she _____ be in America.
I'm not sure about ghosts. They _____ exist.
Roger isn't at school today. He _____ be at home.
That girl speaks fluent German, so she _____ be from Germany.

**c Which modals do we use to express uncertainty?
Which modal do we use to express negative certainty?
Which modal do we use to express positive certainty?
Which form of the verb do we use after modals?**

5 First conditional

a Look at these sentences.

If interest rates fall, I'll borrow the money.
If you don't eat enough, you'll lose too much weight.

b Complete these sentences.

If she _____ late, I _____ to the cinema without her.
If it _____ sunny on Saturday, I _____ to the seaside.

**c Which tense do you use in the *if* clause?
Which tense do you use in the other half of the sentence?**

NB 1 When *if* means *whenever*, you can use the present tense in both halves of the sentence.

Example
If I visit my grandmother, I take her a bunch of flowers.

2 You can NEVER use the future tense in the *if* clause.

UNIT 26

WHAT HAPPENED TO YOU?

🎧 80 ▶ **Listen.**

It's Sunday morning. Carol is phoning her friend Bob. She had a party on Saturday evening and Bob didn't come. She wants to find out why.

BOB Hello, 607 7015.

CAROL Hello, it's Carol Manning here. Can I speak to Bob, please?

BOB Speaking. Hi, Carol. I expect you're ringing to find out what happened last night, aren't you?

CAROL Well, yes. We were all waiting for you. I wanted you to meet some of my new friends. What happened to you?

BOB It's a long story, Carol. I left the house in plenty of time to get to you. I knew I had to get the number 75 bus but when I got to the bus stop, the bus had already gone.

CAROL But I said you could catch the 82 bus as well, or even the train. Why didn't you do that?

BOB Well, that's where the trouble really started. I looked in my pocket for the instructions you'd written for me but I'd lost them. So I decided to phone Barbara and ask her to meet me so we could come together.

CAROL And what happened then? Barbara didn't come to the party either.

BOB No, of course she didn't. She was with me!

CAROL Tell me more!

BOB Well, we met at The Three Bells and waited for another bus to come. We waited for about twenty minutes and then, because it still hadn't arrived, we decided to walk to the station to see if there was a train. As we were walking past Brown's department store we saw a woman run out shouting 'Stop! Thief!' She was chasing a man of about twenty-four or twenty-five.

CAROL Sounds pretty exciting.

BOB Anyway, I ran after him but before I caught up with him the police arrived and stopped him.

CAROL What happened then?

BOB Well, they wanted to know exactly what had happened so we all spent the next two hours at the police station.

CAROL So I suppose it was too late to come then?

BOB Yes, it was ten o'clock. We intended to come anyway and tell you the whole story but . . .

CAROL I can guess the rest. The last bus had already left!

BOB I'm really sorry, Carol. We couldn't phone, of course, because you're not on the phone yet. You will ask us another time, won't you?

CAROL I'll have to see about that . . .

Put these facts in order. Write *1, 2, 3,* **etc.**

_____ Bob went to the bus stop but he missed the bus.
_____ They waited for the next bus.
_____ He phoned Barbara.
_____ They chased a thief.
_____ He met Barbara at The Three Bells.
_____ They went to the police station.
_____ They walked past Brown's department store.
_____ They missed the last bus.

36

1 *Language* Focus

BOB When I got to the bus stop, the bus had already gone.

BOB I looked in my pocket for the instructions you'd written for me but I'd lost them.

BOB Because the bus still hadn't arrived, we decided to walk to the station.

BOB They wanted to know exactly what had happened.

🎧 81 ▶ **Listen.**

Now complete these sentences.

1 When I (arrive), she (go) to bed.

_____

2 I (want) to phone but I (lose) your number.

_____

3 His mother (ask) him what he (do).

🎧 82 ▶ **Listen and check your answers.**

2 ... the lesson had started

1 Complete the sentences to describe these illustrations.

Example

When I got to school, *the lesson had started*.

1 When I arrived at the station,_____
_____.

2 _____ before I arrived.

3 She wanted to know where I _____.

4 He arrived after the match _____.

Check your answers with another student.

 2 Listen to these people discussing others they were at school with. They had a reunion in 1985 and are going to meet up again this year.

Student A Fill in the information for Jack Beecham, Tim Brown and Margaret Green. Give this information to Student B.
Student B Fill in the information for Ann Smith, Tom Margam and Ian Blythe. Give this information to Student A.

	AFTER SCHOOL	CAREER
Jack Beecham		
Tim Brown		
Margaret Green		
Ann Smith		
Tom Margam		
Ian Blythe		

When you have finished choose one of the people and write a paragraph about what he or she had done. Begin like this:

By the time they met in 1985 Ann Smith... She had...

3 Story writing

1 Work in groups. Look at the vocabulary below, choose some of the words and use them in a story leading up to the man's arrival at his office. One person in the group should write the story.

diversion delayed shot traffic motorway accident bank helicopters police stopped unconscious snow cup of coffee upset hospital flowers surprised first aid

Begin like this:

Murray Smith left his house at the usual time but hadn't gone far before he noticed...

2 When you have finished, read your story to another group. Are your stories similar?

WB 26.1–2

3 Write out the other group's story.

🎧 84 ▸ **Listen and read.**

LEAVE THIS TO ME!

True or false?

1 Sue is Jo's sister.
2 Dave is Sue's boyfriend.
3 Sue doesn't want to go out with Dave.
4 Sue phones Dave.
5 Dave answers the phone.
6 Sue sees Dave arrive before Jo.
7 Dave hears Jo's telephone conversation.
 8 Jo is very embarrassed.

4 Language Focus

(SUE I can't come.)
JO Sue says she can't come.

(SUE I've got too much homework.)
JO She says that she's got too much homework.

(SUE I had a very hard day at school today.)
JO She says she had a very hard day at school today.

(SUE I'll speak to him tomorrow.)
JO She says she'll speak to him tomorrow.

🎧 85 ▸ **Listen.**

Now put Dave's words into reported speech.

(DAVE I'm fed up with Sue.)

JOHN He says _____

(DAVE She promised to go out with me.)

JOHN He says that _____

(DAVE I'm not going to go out with her again.)

JOHN He says _____

(DAVE I'll speak to her tomorrow.)

JOHN He says _____

NB The use of *that* in these sentences is optional.

🎧 86 ▸ **Listen and check your answers.**

5 Despatch riders

WE REQUIRE EXPERIENCED/INEXPERIENCED
DESPATCH RIDERS
CITY BASED ● FULL TRAINING GIVEN ● RADIO SUPPLIED
● NO FEES ● HIGH EARNINGS
01–608 0883
Member of the Despatch Association

You and your partner are the managers of Bullet Despatch. Choose a despatch rider.

1
Student A Read the letters of application from Mike Lees and Susan Watson.
Student B Read the letters of application from Peter Bull and Arthur Eastment.

253, South Parade,
Kingston,
Surrey.

15/3/89

Dear Madam or Sir,
I would like to apply for the post of despatch rider advertised in the paper last Saturday. I'm twenty years old and I left school when I was sixteen. I got a job as a despatch rider with Mercury Express in London when I left school and I worked for them for three years. I had an accident last year and I had to stop work, but I'm OK now. I have a lot of experience as a despatch rider. Unfortunately I haven't got a bike at the moment.

Yours sincerely,

Mike Lees

16,Marchmont Road,
Twickenham,
Middlesex.

16th March 1989

Dear Sir or Madam,
I am writing to apply for the post of despatch rider with your company. I am nineteen years old and I've worked as a despatch rider in Bristol for the last two years. I am a good rider - last year I passed my advanced rider's motorcycle test - and I own a Suzuki 750 motorcycle. I moved here last month so I am beginning to get to know London quite well.

Yours faithfully,

Susan Watson

Susan Watson

79 Thorpe Street
Surbiton
Surrey
17/3/89

Dear Sir
I am applying for the job of despatch rider with your company. I'm seventeen years old and I've just left school. I've got five GCSE's. I bought a motorcycle last year and passed my test last March. I'm a very good rider. I've got a Honda 125 motorcycle now. I know London quite well — I've lived here for five years. Hoping to hear from you soon.
Yours sincerely
Peter Bull

13 Bromley Road
Catford
London

15th March 1989

Dear Sirs,
I saw your ad for despatch riders in <u>Bike</u> magazine last month and I would like to apply. I am sixteen years old and I am still at school and I'm looking for a part time job as a despatch rider. I haven't passed my test yet, but I'm taking it next month. I haven't got my own bike but I can borrow my friend's Kawasaki. I know London very well.
Yours faithfully,

Arthur Eastment

Arthur Eastment

2 Fill in the chart for your candidates.

Name	Age	Owns bike?	Experience	Knows London?
Peter Bull				
Mike Lees				
Arthur Eastment				
Susan Watson				

3 Tell your partner about your candidates.
Example
STUDENT A What does Peter Bull say?
STUDENT B He says he's seventeen years old ...

Make notes about your partner's candidates.

4 Choose the best candidate together.

6 Old and young

1 Work in groups.

Groups A Write four sentences about young people from the point of view of old people. Begin
Old people say that young people ...

Groups B Write four sentences about old people from the point of view of young people. Begin
Young people say that old people ...

Read your sentences to another group. Write down theirs as they read them to you.

🎧 87 **2 Listen to this old man and young woman discussing old and young people. Make notes.**

Now write sentences reporting what they say.

Example
The old man says that young people are ...

3 Discuss the views of the people you heard. Compare them with yours.

WB 26.3–4

1 Skills Focus: Reading

1 Before you read the article, discuss these questions.

1 Are there any sports which women don't usually play?
2 Is there any logical reason why they don't play them?
3 Women: Have you ever been excluded from playing something by men?
4 Men: Have you ever stopped women taking part in any sport because they were women?

2 Who are these people? Read the text quickly and find out.

1 Sallie Jackson
2 Shauna Williams
3 Flo Bilton
4 Ted Croker
5 Linda Whitehead

FAIR PLAY FOR WOMEN'S FOOTBALL

The Football Association has always been rather traditional in its administration of the game. In 1921 its members elected to ban women from playing football; they didn't say women were not capable of playing football, just that they wouldn't be allowed to play on proper pitches with qualified officials in any organised way. And once in force that rule was rigidly applied for 49 years.

What broke down the resistance of the F.A. to women's football was the 1966 World Cup. Female teams began to appear everywhere and within three years established sides were operating in structured leagues. The Women's Football Association was formed in 1969 with 51 clubs as members, and the F.A. revoked its infamous ban in 1970 in the face of strong W.F.A. representation.

Other countries followed Britain's example and in 1971 international football bodies F.I.F.A. and U.E.F.A. decided that their members must not only recognise the women's game but take steps to see that it be properly controlled. The first England International women's side was picked in 1972 and won its first game (against Scotland) 3–2. The W.F.A. has now got a domestic membership of 200 clubs playing in 23 leagues.

Managers of men's clubs often complain about foreign clubs buying their best players. Well, the same thing happens in women's football. In Italy they play women's soccer professionally and have bought many of our star players. Sallie Jackson of Fulham and Millwall's Shauna Williams are two of our best players who have gone to play in Italy. 'When a woman has no prospect of getting a job, and is offered the chance to do something she loves – and get paid for it – who can blame her?' commented league official Flo Bilton.

You may have seen recent stories about girls who are star players in their boys' school team being dropped for important matches because the F.A. won't allow them to play. F.A. Secretary Ted Croker is coming under increasing pressure from girl players who are angry at being dropped after being picked on merit.

At senior level women's football differs from the men's game in that the emphasis is on skill rather than strength, on stylish play instead of aggression. Apart from that it is remarkably similar – with the same complaints about fouls, foul language on the pitch, and foul pitches... The good news is that wherever you live you can find a team and get a game. Anyone wanting to play or watch should contact Ms Linda Whitehead, Secretary, Women's Football Association, 11 Portsea Mews, Portsea Place, London W2 2BN. Tel. 01–402 9388.

3 Work in pairs.
Find these words in the text. Translate them into your language. Don't use a dictionary! Compare translations with another pair of students.

ban	pitches
rule	league
picked	blame
dropped	skill
strength	foul (3 meanings)
on merit	aggression

4 In which paragraph do you find information about

1 girls being dropped from matches because the F.A. won't allow them to play? _____
2 the result of the first international match that the first English women's team played? _____
3 the date of the original ban of women from football? _____
4 the similarities between women's and men's football? _____
5 the date when the W.F.A. was formed? _____
6 women who go to play abroad because they have no work in England? _____

5 True or false?

1 The F.A. banned women from playing football because they said they were not good enough.
2 The 1966 World Cup changed men's attitudes to women in football.
3 The W.F.A. forced the F.A. to allow women to play football in 1970.
4 Britain was the first country to have a women's football association.
5 Italian clubs often buy English women players.
6 Flo Filton is angry at women who go to play abroad.
7 Girls cannot play in boys' school teams.
8 Men play football more aggressively than women.

2 Skills Focus: Listening

You are going to hear an interview with Michelle Quacoe, a professional footballer. Look at the list of questions. Which would you ask if you were the interviewer? Put ticks (√).

YOU   INTERVIEWER

_____ _____ 1 Do you play any other sports?

_____ _____ 2 Which team do you usually play for?

_____ _____ 3 Which position do you usually play in?

_____ _____ 4 Did you have trouble getting a game when you first started?

_____ _____ 5 Were you ever excluded from playing in teams because you were a woman?

_____ _____ 6 What do you think of women who play abroad?

_____ _____ 7 When did you start playing football?

_____ _____ 8 Have you ever played abroad yourself?

_____ _____ 9 Are women more aggressive than men when they play football?

_____ _____ 10 Are there many professional women's teams in Britain now?

_____ _____ 11 How much does a top woman footballer earn?

🎧 88 ▷ **Now listen to the interview and tick the questions that the interviewer asks.**

▲39 **Listen again. Make notes of Michelle's answers.**

3 Vocabulary Development

Using a monolingual dictionary

During the year your teacher has probably told you that it is a good idea to use a monolingual dictionary. This section will help you understand why. You will also learn how to make the best use of your dictionary.

1 Read the dictionary entry, which gives several meanings for the word *foul*. **You had to find three meanings for this word in exercise 3 of Skills Focus: Reading.**

foul /faʊl/, **fouler, foulest; fouls, fouling, fouled. 1** If something is **foul, 1.1** it is unpleasant because it is dirty or decayed. EG *The water in the pools became tepid and foul... We spent a grim night in a very foul cabin.* **1.2** it is unpleasant and not at all enjoyable or successful. EG *I've had a really foul day at work... It's such foul luck for you all.* **1.3** it is evil and wicked. EG *...a foul crime.* [ADJ QUALIT = filthy] [ADJ QUALIT = rotten] [ADJ QUALIT = base, vile]

2 If you say that you will do something **by fair means or foul,** you are prepared to use any means at all in order to get what you want and you do not care if your behaviour is dishonest and unfair. [PHR : USED AS AN A]

3 Foul weather is unpleasant, windy, and stormy with a lot of rain or snow. [ADJ QUALIT ⇑ bad]

4 Foul language is offensive and contains unacceptable words such as swear words and rude words related to sex or other bodily functions. EG *I won't have you using such foul language in my house!* ▸ used of people who use foul language, or of their way of thinking. EG *What a foul mind you've got!* [ADJ QUALIT ⇑ bad = coarse, obscene] [▸ = filthy]

5 If someone has a **foul** temper, they become angry or violent very suddenly and easily. [ADJ QUALIT : USU ATTRIB]

6 If you **fall foul of** someone, or if you **run foul of** them, you do something which makes them angry or annoyed with you. EG *He was found drowned in a river after falling foul of local poachers.* [PHR : VB INFLECTS ⇑ anger]

7 If you **foul** something, **7.1** you make it dirty. EG *The deck would soon be fouled with the blood from their backs... ...a tern lying on a beach, fouled by oil.* **7.2** you drop faeces onto it. EG *...an elector who was complaining about dogs fouling the pavement.* [V+O = soil] [V+O = soil]

8 If something **fouls** a mechanism, device, net, etc it accidentally becomes twisted or knotted around it and prevents it from working properly. EG *The boat's engine stopped because some weed had fouled the propeller... They fouled their nets on these underwater obstructions... Suddenly the rope started coming too fast. It fouled on the winch.* [V-ERG ⇑ block = snag]

9 If a player **fouls** in a game or sport, or if they **foul** another player, they do something which is not allowed according to the rules. [V OR V+O]

10 A **foul** is an act in a game of sport that is not allowed according to the rules. EG *The England team's record of fouls was among the worst.* ▸ used as an adjective. EG *If the white ball goes into a pocket in snooker, it is a foul shot.* [N COUNT ⇑ infringement] [▸ ADJ CLASSIF : ATTRIB ≠ acceptable]

foul up. If you **foul up** something such as a plan, you spoil it by doing something wrong or stupid; used in informal English. EG *So many good projects have been fouled up by elementary mistakes in planning.* [PHRASAL VB : V + O + ADV ⇑ ruin = mess up]
● See also **foul-up.**

2 The numbers indicate the different meanings of the word. In the margin are abbreviations of names of parts of speech: noun (N), verb (V), adjective (ADJ), adverb (ADV), etc.

What part of speech is *foul* **the first time it appears in the article? Which dictionary definition gives you its meaning?**

The second and third times *foul* **appears it is an adjective. Look at the definitions for the adjective** *foul*. **Which one describes language? Which one could describe the state of a football pitch?**

3 The dictionary also gives synonyms of words. What synonym(s) does it give for *foul*

1 as a noun?

2 as an adjective describing language?

3 as an adjective describing the state of something, e.g. a football pitch?

4 Look at the dictionary entry again. Can you find these things?

1 The phonetic transcription of the word.

2 The comparative and superlative forms of the adjective.

3 The plural of the noun.

4 The gerund and the simple past of the verb.

5 A synonym for *foul weather*.

WB 27.1–4

The Royal Family

HOW **HARD** DOES IT WORK?

by Tim Madge

IN a survey which asked young people about their attitudes to the royal family, many said they thought its members were hardworking, while others said they were 'boring people who just prance about doing nothing'.

There was a big difference between boys and girls over how much they were interested in the royal family in the first place. Over half (52 per cent) of girls said that they were interested in the royal family but only 34 per cent of boys said that they were.

Opinions about Princess Diana seem to vary. One girl said she wore 'awful clothes' while another thought she was 'perfect'. But most people liked her for her dress sense and more people liked her than disliked her.

Half the people interviewed were very positive about the Queen and thought she worked very hard. Only 24 per cent wanted the royal family changed in any way. But many people had no idea what the royal family were supposed to be doing. Ten per cent thought that they were 'professional visitors' at events or functions, 9 per cent

		Engagement	Days abroad	Total
1	The Queen	860	39	899
2	Princess Anne	802	22	824
3	Prince Charles	602	40	642
4	Prince Philip	514	98	612
5	Princess Diana	352	26	378
6	The Queen Mother	254	—	254
7	Princess Margaret	196	12	208
8	Prince Andrew	122	8	130
9	Prince Edward	96	—	96
10	Duchess of York (Fergie)	92	3	95

said they were national symbols, 8 per cent said they were 'official' tourists and 5 per cent said they were ambassadors for Britain. Thirteen per cent believed that they ruled the country or 'looked after it'.

Many of the people interviewed thought that the royal family worked very hard, especially the Queen. Fifty per cent thought she was hardworking. Next came Princess Anne and Prince Charles (29 per cent each), Princess Diana (25 per cent), Prince Andrew (18 per cent), and the Queen Mother (17 per cent).

Some people (24 per cent) said that Prince Edward was the laziest, slightly fewer (22 per cent) thought this of Princess Margaret, while still fewer (19 per cent) thought Princess Michael did least. In contrast, Princess Anne was admired for her charity work and sense of humour, while the Duchess of York (Fergie) was liked for her naturalness and friendliness. Some people were not so positive. They said that the royal family should 'pay their own national health contributions and taxes'.

From the Guardian, 29 April 1987

True or false?

1 More girls were interested in the royal family than boys.
2 Most people disliked Princess Diana's clothes.
3 Everybody thought the Queen worked very hard.
4 Many young people don't know what the function of the royal family is.
5 Many people thought that Princess Anne was very lazy.
6 The Duchess of York is natural and friendly.
7 Members of the royal family don't pay taxes.

 40

1 Language Focus

Many people thought that the members of the royal family were hardworking.
One girl said that Princess Diana wore awful clothes.
Over half the girls said that they were interested in the royal family.
Half the people thought the Queen worked very hard.
Some people said that Prince Edward was the laziest.

 Listen.

 Now listen to these people talking about the royal family.

Dawn
I like the Queen and the Queen Mother but I don't like Princess Anne.

Geoff
I like Prince Charles because he has done a lot of good work with young people.

Teresa
I don't like the royal family very much. They cost the country too much money!

Clive
I'm not really interested in the royal family. I think they are quite boring people.

Report what they said.

1 Dawn said that _____

_____ .

2 Geoff said that _____

_____ .

3 Teresa said that _____

_____ .

4 Clive said that _____

_____ .

2 TV survey

Ann McLoughlin asked three people their opinions of British TV. She asked them these questions.

Which TV channel do you prefer?
Which programmes do you like?
Which programmes do you not like?
What do you think of advertising on TV?

 Work in groups of three. Each choose one person from the chart. Listen and make notes about his or her opinions. Complete your part of the chart.

	TV CHANNEL	PROGRAMMES		ADVERTISING
		LIKES	DOESN'T LIKE	
Anita				
Paul				
Linda				

Report your answers to the other people in your group.

Example
Anita said that she preferred Channel 4.
She said that she liked documentaries.

Complete the chart.

3 Your own survey

Work in groups. Choose one of these topics.

Advertising on TV   Religion   Modern music
Nuclear energy   Fashion

1 Prepare a list of five questions on your topic. Everyone in the group must write them down.

2 Work in pairs, with a member of another group. Answer each other's questions. Note your partner's answers. Report your findings to your original group.

3 Write a report on the group's findings. Begin like this:

We asked four people about TV advertising. Three said they didn't like advertising on TV, but one person said he liked TV adverts ...

WB 28.1–2

FIRST AID

As its name implies it is the first help given to people suffering from accidents or sudden illness, usually by people with no medical training, while waiting for an ambulance or doctor to arrive. Knowing what to do in an emergency can result in the saving of somebody's life.

● What would you do if there was an accident?
● If someone cut himself badly, would you know what to do?
● If someone fainted, what would you do?

The British Red Cross Society runs first aid courses in most areas of Britain to help people learn what to do in an emergency. If I were you, I'd enrol on one of these before it's too late. The next emergency might involve you or a member of your family.

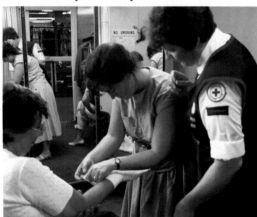

The teacher on one of these courses gave the participants a test on the first day of the course. One of the questions they had to answer was this:

● What would you do if your sister burnt herself badly?

The answers of the participants varied a lot. Here is a selection.

'If my sister burnt herself, I'd put butter on the wound.'
'I'd pour cold water on the wound for at least ten minutes.'
'I'd call an ambulance or take my sister to the hospital.'

By the end of the course all the participants had a much clearer idea of what they should do.

Which answer do you think is the best? Discuss the effects of all the suggested remedies with another student.

Match the words on the left with those on the right.

1 First aid
2 Knowing what to do
3 The British Red Cross Society
4 First aid courses
5 Enrol on one of these courses

runs courses in Britain.
help you know what to do in an emergency.
before it's too late.
is the first help given in an emergency.
can save someone's life.

4 Language Focus

If I were you, I'd enrol on one of these courses.
What would you do if there was an accident?
What would you do if your sister burnt herself badly?
If my sister burnt herself, I'd put butter on the wound.

 Listen.

Now look at the illustrations and choose the most suitable comment for each. Match the words on the left with those on the right.

If I were you,

I'd go to America.

I'd go to bed.

What would you do

If you went to America,

if you saw a ghost?

If I had a lot of money,

you'd see the Statue of Liberty.

 Listen and check your answers.

5 What would you do in an emergency?

In pairs, look at the list of questions and tick (√) the best answers. If you would do something different, write it down.

1 If you witnessed a road accident, would you

_____ a leave the victim where he or she was and try to keep him or her warm?

_____ b move him or her off the road?

_____ c stay and talk to him or her?

d *I would* _____ .

2 If your brother cut himself badly, would you

_____ a put a tight bandage on to stop the bleeding?

_____ b give him a warm drink?

_____ c press on the cut until the bleeding stopped then cover the wound?

d _____ .

3 If your nose was bleeding, would you

_____ a sit down and blow your nose?

_____ b lie down and pinch your nose firmly?

_____ c sit down and pinch your nose firmly?

d _____ .

4 If your mother fainted, would you

_____ a sit her on a chair and put her head between her knees?

_____ b lie her down and lift her legs up?

_____ c lie her down with her head to one side?

d _____ .

5 If your father received an electric shock, would you

_____ a move him from the electric current?

_____ b switch off the electricity and then move him?

_____ c put on a pair of rubber boots and then move him?

d _____ .

6 If there was a small fire in your kitchen, would you

_____ a throw a blanket over it?

_____ b pour water on it?

_____ c get away quickly and close the door?

d _____ .

Discuss your answers with another student.

🎧 94 **Now listen to these people talking about first aid and check your answers.**

6 Unique model competition

Have you ever entered a competition? Have you ever won?

1 Read the advertisement quickly and answer these questions.

1 How long is the modelling contract for?
2 Can you buy the clothes where you like?
3 Where will the finals of the competition be held?
4 What must you send apart from details of your height, size, and colour of hair and eyes?
5 What is important about July 28th?

MODELLING CONTRACT! £500 WORTH OF CLOTHES! £250 CASH! FAME & FORTUNE! TO BE WON IN THE BEAT MODELSEARCH

The BEAT MODELSEARCH enters its second successful month. The standard of entrants has been so high that we are hoping to offer several runners-up modelling contracts!
If you think that like Nadya or Nick Kamen on the left you could be a model, or you know someone who you think could be a model, send us in those snaps now! **Remember we are looking for two models – one male, one female. They will each get:**

● A 12 month modelling contract with new model agency UNIQUE.
● £250 worth of clothes and accessories each from companies such as Ravel and C&A Avanti.
● £125 cash each (and if you're lucky a bottle of vodka or two) from Vladivar.
● The opportunity to appear in a BEAT fashion spread styled by the BLITZ fashion team.

The competition will be judged by a mixture of fashion industry notables, led by Iain R Webb, plus a number of style conscious pop celebrities.

All finalists will be invited to Unique's Chelsea office where they will meet the judges and be photographed by leading fashion photographer Owen Scarbeina.

To enter, all you have to do is send two photographs — one head and shoulders, the other full length — don't worry about the quality, snap shots will do.

Also include details of your height, clothes size, shoe size, hair colour and colour of eyes.

Don't forget to write your name and address on the back and include a SAE if you want your photos back. **Send this to UNIQUE MODEL COMPETITION, THE BEAT, 1 Lower James St, W1. Entries no later than July 28th.**

🎧 95 **2 Colin, Jane and Miranda have decided to enter the competition. Listen to them talking about it. Make notes about how they would spend the prize money if they won and what clothes they would buy.**

3 Imagine that you are going to enter the competition. In groups, discuss what you would do with the money and what clothes you would buy if you won. Make notes.

WB 28.3–5

MOONDOWN

Skills Focus: Reading and Listening

Before you read the next episode, do exercises
1 and 2.

1 Discuss these questions.

1 In Pete's position what would you do?
2 Where do you think Cathy is?

**2 Look at these words from the episode. What
do you think is going to happen?**

flat	address book	*Daily Clarion*
dead	skidded	lorry driver
exploded	brakes	telephone
Linda Markham	address	later

🎧 96 ▶ **Listen and read.**

UNIT 29

EPISODE SIX

Pete is at Cathy's flat.

'Where's her address book? Ah, here it is! Now, what was her name? Linda ... Linda Markham ... here we are. The *Daily Clarion* – 01 823... What's that noise? Who is it? Oh, it's just the newspaper arriving. Huh, the *Westfield Gazette.* Good God! What's this? Jack Sims dead! Oh, no!'

Pete reads the article.

FATAL ACCIDENT ON STAR POINT ROAD

AT six o'clock this evening a car carrying two passengers, a man and a woman, skidded off the road near Star Point. The car exploded when it hit a tree and the occupants were killed instantly.

The driver of the car has been named as Jack Sims, aged 55, a lorry driver from Westfield.

The other occupant of the car, a woman in her mid-twenties, has not yet been identified. The fire that broke out when the car exploded has made it difficult to identify her.

The cause of the accident is not yet known, although police suspect that the car's brakes may have failed.

Mr Graham Brooke, the director of Moondown power station where Jack Sims worked, said: 'We are all shocked by this terrible tragedy. Jack was a good man and a hard worker.'

'Oh no! Poor Cathy! I must telephone Linda and get her here, then we'll go to the police. They won't get away with this! Where's that number?

'Hello, the *Daily Clarion*? I'd like to speak to Linda Markham, please. Yes, that's right! Hello? Linda Markham? I'm Pete Chisman, Cathy's friend. Yes, I've just heard about the accident. It's in the local paper. I think Cathy was probably in the car. Can you get here as soon as possible? Good! Come to my flat. The address is 34 Courtmeade Close, Westfield. It's opposite the bus station. OK, see you later. Bye!

'Wait a minute. Brooke ... I know that name! No, it can't be!'

3 Write questions about the newspaper article.

1 What _____?
2 When _____?
3 Where _____?
4 Who _____?
5 Why _____?

Exchange questions with another student. Answer his or her questions.

4 Answer these questions.

1 Who is Linda Markham?
2 Pete is frightened at the beginning of the episode. How can you tell?
3 What is the name of the director of Moondown?
4 What does Pete think has happened to Cathy?
5 Why does Pete phone Linda Markham?
6 Does Pete know Linda?
7 Has Linda heard about the accident?

 8 Has Linda been to Pete's flat before?

5 Before you listen to the second part of the episode, read these sentences and decide if they are true or false.

1 Linda Markham arrives at the flat.
2 A policeman arrives after a few minutes.
3 Pete tells the story of their investigations.
4 Pete thinks that Jack Sims's car crash was an accident.
5 Mr Eastwood found out from Jack Sims that Cathy and Pete were at Star Point on Saturday night.
6 Brooke is Mr Eastwood's uncle.
7 Mr Eastwood phones Pete at the end of the episode.

 Now listen and check your answers.

WB 29.1–2

Skills Focus: Writing
Formal Letters (2)

In Unit 10 you learned how to lay out a formal letter. Look back at that unit now to remind yourself of the way to do this. In that unit you learned how to write a formal letter applying for a job. In this unit you will learn how to write a formal letter asking for further information about something. The basic layout is the same for both letters.

1 Read the advertisement for an Amstrad study holiday in Scotland. Find this information.

1 In what part of Scotland does the course take place?
2 Is it necessary to have group tuition?
3 Does the price for the two-day course (£89) include accommodation?
4 Is the cost of accommodation inclusive of meals?

TUITION   **AMSTRAD 8256/8512**

Join us in the Scottish Borders and learn word-processing on the AMSTRAD 8256/8512. Combine tuition with a holiday in one of Scotland's loveliest areas. We offer warm, comfortable accommodation and home cooking in our beautifully situated guest house.

Courses can be tailored to suit your requirements. Individual tuition guaranteed. If you require instruction on some other application, please call me and enquire.

Prices: £89 for two-day course
£45 for one-day course
£8.50 per hour (by arrangement)
Accommodation: £16 per day full board
Send for free leaflet and application form to:
**GARY HALL The Lodge, Sidmount Avenue,
MOFFAT DG10 9BS Tel: (0683) 20440**

---

2 This is the letter which Mike Smith wrote after he had read the advertisement. Read it carefully.

64, Morton Road,
Liverpool.
June 30th 1988

Mr Gary Hall,
The Lodge,
Sidmount Avenue,
Moffat DG10 9BS.

Dear Mr Hall,
I saw your advertisement in the June edition of Your Amstrad magazine. I have recently bought an Amstrad 8512 word processor and am interested in understanding more about it.
Do you think you could send me a free leaflet and application form? Could you also tell me if you have courses in August and September?
I enclose a stamped addressed envelope for your reply.

Yours sincerely,

Mike Smith

Now answer these questions.

1 There are at least four things about the letter that show that it is formal. What are they?
2 There are two examples of a formal way of asking for something. What are they?
3 Why do you think Mike Smith wants to do the course?
4 In which paragraph does he refer to the advertisement? In which paragraph does he ask for more information?
5 Does the letter contain any information which is not necessary?
6 Why does he enclose an envelope with his address and a stamp on it?

3 Look at these advertisements. Choose one and write a letter asking for further information. Use the letter opposite as a model.

MARLBOROUGH COLLEGE SUMMER SCHOOL
17 July-6 August
A RELAXED YET STIMULATING HOLIDAY

Over 70 different weekly residential/non-residential courses for families or individuals ranging from Art, Architecture and Bridge to Wine Appreciation, Woodcrafts and Yoga. With special Children's Activities, 7-13 and 13-16 years. Plus evening entertainments. For brochure:

The Secretary, Marlborough College Summer School, Marlborough, Wilts SN8 1PA, or phone (0672) 53888, 24 hours.

The Wildlife Safari Experience in Kenya & Tanzania

Inclusive Safaris of exceptional quality and unbeatable value from Kenya's largest family owned Safari company

- Luxurious accommodation
- Custom designed fleet of "Safari Cruisers"
- Personalised Safari planning

Colour brochure and video from:
Wildlife Safari
Freepost 35
LONDON
W1E 5QZ
01-439 3938
(24 hrs)
Quote Ref. KEN

HILLS & DALES UK
ACTIVITY HOLIDAYS

For further details of Hills and Dales UK Activity Holidays please contact:—
Office: Hills & Dales UK
        5 Beaufort Grove,
        Morecambe,
        Lancashire,
        LA4 6UF ENGLAND
        Telephone: 0524 422487 (24 Hours)

LEISURELY CYCLING
in beautiful English Lakeland as seen on T.V. Choice of good Hotels, Guest Homes. 7 day price choice from £126/£260. 'All luggage transported.' Free days. Highly recom. for all age groups. Col. Broch.
CYCLORAMA HOLIDAYS
GRANGE HOTEL
Grange-over-Sands (1),
Cumbria, LA11 6EJ
Tel: (04484) 3666.

TENNIS HOLIDAYS
Weekends/5 days/7 days. Expert coaching / play. 18 outdoor/indoor courts. Full accom. Heated pool. 9 hole par 3 golf course. 20 lovely acres. Near Eastbourne/sea. Col Broch.
Windmill Hill Place Tennis Resort, Dept O, Hailsham, E. Sussex. (0323) 832552

1 Talking about an earlier past

a **In pairs, choose statements and make comments.**

Example

STUDENT A When my sister came home she was really miserable.
STUDENT B Why?
STUDENT A She'd failed her exams.

1 When she came home from her holidays she was really happy.
2 They arrested the man that night.
3 Everything I took out of the washing machine was blue.
4 They took her to the hospital immediately.
5 I didn't think I would see him again!
6 She wasn't there when he phoned.
7 I didn't realise it was Mary at first.

b **When you have finished, choose four exchanges and write them out.**

2 Reporting what people say

Write a short description of yourself on a piece of paper.

Example

I'm a girl. I'm sixteen years old, I'm quite tall and I've got short brown hair. My hobbies are dancing and playing tennis.

Give your piece of paper to your teacher, who will mix it with everyone else's and give one back to you. Report what's on your piece of paper to the rest of the class.

Example

She's a girl and she says she's sixteen years old. She says she's quite tall and she says she's got short brown hair. She says her hobbies are dancing and playing tennis.

The rest of the class have to guess the name of the person.

3 Reporting what people said

Memory Game
Read what these three friends said about music. You have two minutes.

Neil 'I like rock music, and my favourite singers are Mick Jagger and Tina Turner. I've got lots of cassettes and I listen to them every day. I never listen to the radio because I don't like very modern pop music. It's all the same.'

Melanie 'I only like classical music, especially Bach. I haven't got a stereo or a walkman, but I've got a radio, so I listen to that a lot. I always listen to music in the evenings when I'm doing my homework.'

Heather 'I like jazz and folk music. I play the guitar and I like singing, too. Sometimes I invite my friends to my house and we sing and play together. I've got a good stereo and a large collection of records and compact discs.'

Work in pairs. Close your books and write down what the three people said.

Example
Neil said he liked rock music.

Read your answers to another student. Check them in the book. The person with the most correct answers is the winner.

4 Talking about future possibilities (2)

What would you do if you
saw two people fighting?
found a snake in your house?
had the chance to go to the States for a year?
saw somebody stealing from a shop?
had an accident driving your father's or mother's car?

Write your answers, then ask another student. Would you do the same thing?

5 Vocabulary

These are some of the words you needed in Units 26–30. Do you know them now? Choose ten and write sentences to show you understand their meanings.

upset	unconscious	emergency
apply	not feel	faint
move	very well	bandage
lazy	get to know	illness
advert	hardworking	sense of
blame	strength	humour

🎧 98 6 Pronunciation

Look at these words.

1 out   2 serious   3 four

Listen and repeat. Listen especially to the pronunciation of the letters *ou* in each case.

Now look at these words and decide which category they belong to. Write *1, 2* or *3*.

hour _____	course _____
bought _____	colour _____
found _____	your _____
unconscious _____	house _____
court _____	curious _____
loud _____	mouth _____

Listen and check your answers.

How do you do these things in English? Write a sentence for each function.

1 Tell someone what had happened by the time you got to the party.

_____

2 Tell someone what you would do if you saw an accident.

_____

3 Report what someone else says he is doing.

_____

4 Report what someone said about a TV programme.

_____

1 Past perfect

a Look at these sentences.

When I got to the bus stop the bus had already left.
The detective saw footsteps where someone had walked in the flowerbed.
After waiting half an hour I went home because he still hadn't arrived.

b Complete these sentences.

At the station I realised I

_____ _____ my

wallet at home.

I gave the book to my

brother but he _____

_____ it already.

By the time I arrived at his

office the meeting

_____ _____ .

c Does the past perfect action happen before or after the simple past action? Sometimes we can use the simple past or the past perfect. Which must we use when it is important to show an action was completed before another began?

2 Reported speech (1)

a Look at these sentences.

She says she can't come to the phone because she's having a bath.
He says that he's doing his homework.

b Complete these sentences.

She _____ that she

_____ any money so

she can't go to the cinema

this evening.

He _____ he's

_____ a football match

on TV, so he doesn't want to talk to you now.

c In (a), what do the girl and boy actually say? What is the tense of the verb *say*? Does the tense of a sentence change when it is reported in this way? Is it necessary to use *that* in reported speech?

3 Reported speech (2)

a Look at these sentences.

Michael said he liked the royal family, especially the Queen.
Rachel's parents said that they didn't enjoy going to the theatre very much.

b Complete these sentences.

She _____ that she

_____ to buy a car.

They _____ that they

_____ to a party that

evening.

c In (a), what did Michael say? What did Rachel's parents say? What is the tense of the verb *say*? Does the tense of a sentence change when it is reported in this way?

4 Second conditional

a Look at these sentences.

If he gave me a lot of money, I'd buy a new car.
If I were you, I'd go to bed.
If I saw a snake, I'd kill it.

b Complete these sentences.

If I _____ a lot of

money, I _____ to the

States.

If someone _____

unconscious, I _____

artificial respiration.

If I _____ you, I

_____ to the doctor.

c Which tense do you use in the *if* clause? Which tense do you use in the main clause? Look at the information about the first conditional in Unit 23. Which conditional do you use to express a possible state of affairs and its probable result? Which conditional do you use to express a more unlikely state of affairs and its probable result?

DIEGO ARMANDO MARADONA

Where was Maradona born?
How long has he been playing football?
How long has he been living in Italy?

Read the article and find out more about this world famous footballer.

Diego Armando Maradona is one of a family of eight children and was born on October 30th 1960. He's been playing football since he was a very small boy. He played his first games in the back streets of Villa Fiorito, a poor suburb of Buenos Aires. His outstanding talent was soon recognised and he was invited to join the Argentinos Juniors team. He stayed with them until he went to Spain in 1982, where he joined Barcelona. He was with Barcelona for two seasons and played with distinction, although he suffered from injury and illness. He's been living in Italy since 1984 and playing for Naples. When someone asked him how long he was going to stay in Italy Maradona answered: 'I've been living here for several years now and I'm working with a good team. At the moment I can't say how long I'll stay.' Since he joined Naples they've been working well together and doing very well in the championship tables. In 1986 Maradona played for Argentina in the World Cup, leading them to victory and showing himself to be the most brilliant individual player of the tournament.

Find statements in the text to justify these comments.

1 Maradona comes from a large family.
2 Maradona's family wasn't rich.
3 Maradona was very young when he played for Argentinos Juniors.
4 Maradona was not in good health when he was in Spain.
5 Maradona stayed in Spain for two years.
6 Argentina won the World Cup in 1986.

44

1 Language Focus

How long has he been playing football?
He's been playing football since he was a very small boy.
How long has he been living in Italy?
He's been living in Italy since 1984.

I've been living here for several years now.
I've been working with a good team.
They've been working well.
He's been playing for Naples since 1984.

 99 **Listen.**

Now complete the dialogue.

INTERVIEWER   How long have you been living in your present house?

YOU   *I've been living in my house …* _____ .

INTERVIEWER   And how long have you been attending this school?

YOU   _____ .

INTERVIEWER   How long have you been studying English?

YOU   _____ .

INTERVIEWER   How long have you been doing this exercise?

YOU   _____ .

Practise the dialogue with another student.

2 What have you been doing?

Write sentences using *I've been* with an expression from A and an expression from B.

A	B
studying Latin	for half an hour
reading this book	since I was very young
doing my homework	for ten years
living in my house	since four o'clock
watching TV	for three hours
playing the piano	since I was born
waiting for my friend	for a long time

Work in groups of three. Guess how long people have been doing the things in A. You get one point for every correct answer.

Example

STUDENT A   I've been studying Latin.
STUDENT B   I think he's been studying Latin for a long time.
STUDENT C   How long have you been studying Latin?
STUDENT A   For a long time. **(One point for Student B.)**

Take turns to make the statements. The winner is the one with most points.

3 Group stories

1 In groups, make up a story. Begin like this:

'It's now two o'clock in the morning and we're exhausted! We've been …'

You will get some ideas from the pictures but use your own ideas too.

Tell your story to the rest of the class.

2 Write out the story you liked best.

WB 31.1–2

UNIT 31

Plans for the end-of-term party

 Listen.

Karen, Julie and Stuart are talking outside school about their end-of-term party.

KAREN So, what about this weekend? What did your mother say about you coming to the party?

JULIE It's no good, Karen. I can't come.

STUART Why not? Everybody's going. It's our end-of-term party.

JULIE No, it's no good. She always makes me come home by ten o'clock and the party doesn't start until half past eight.

STUART Can't you persuade her as it's the end of term?

KAREN Why don't you stay the night with me? Then she won't be worried about you.

JULIE No, she won't let me do that. I'd like to come but . . .

STUART Oh, come on. I'm sure we can make her change her mind.

KAREN Your mother's friendly with David's mum, isn't she?

JULIE Well, yes . . . Why?

KAREN We can ask David's mum to speak to her. David's coming.

JULIE She won't change her mind. She says she wants me to look after my brother on Saturday.

STUART She's impossible! She doesn't let you do anything!

KAREN Oh, don't be silly, Stuart. Do your parents let you do everything you want to?

STUART Er . . . no. But . . .

KAREN Well, be a bit more reasonable then. Julie's parents have their reasons, I expect. I think we should ask David's mum to speak to her. What do you think, Julie?

JULIE We could try, I suppose. I'll give her a ring this evening.

KAREN I hope you can come. It'll be fun.

JULIE I hope so, too. I really do.

Complete the paragraph.

The students in Karen, Julie and Stuart's class are having a _____ at the _____ because it's the _____ of _____. _____ says she can't go. The party is starting at _____ and she usually has to be _____ at ten o'clock. They are going to phone _____'s mum. She is a _____ of Julie's mum, and they hope she can make Julie's mum change her mind.

104

45

4 Language Focus

JULIE She always makes me come home by ten o'clock.

JULIE She says she wants me to look after my brother on Saturday.

STUART She doesn't let you do anything!

KAREN Do your parents let you do everything you want to?

 Listen.

David's mum spoke to Julie's mum the next day. What happened? Guess. Put a tick (✓) next to the statements you think are true.

_____ Julie's mum let her go to the party.

_____ Julie's mum didn't let her go to the party.

_____ Julie's mum wanted her to look after her brother.

_____ Julie's mum wanted her to stay with Karen.

_____ Julie's mum made her come home at eleven o'clock.

 Listen to David's mum and Julie's mum talking. Check your answers.

5 Parent power

Answer the questions in the column YOU. Ask another student the questions and put his or her answers in the column YOUR PARTNER.

	YOU	YOUR PARTNER
Do your parents let you		
stay out late?		
go to discos?		
invite friends home?		
drink alcohol?		
smoke?		
choose your own clothes?		
Do they make you		
keep your room tidy?		
stay at home and study?		
go out with them at weekends?		
lay the table?		
go shopping with them?		
Do they want you		
to get high marks at school?		
to go to university?		
to leave school and get a job?		
to get a job in the holidays?		
to do the same things as your brother/sister?		
to become independent?		

6 Teenagers

1 What is life like for teenagers in other countries? A group of foreign students was interviewed by the magazine _Teen_. In groups of three, listen and make notes about what their parents let them do (Student A), make them do (Student B) and want them to do (Student C).

	Coming home at night	Work/Career
Jesus		
Miwa		
Dominic		
Maria Paula		

2 Tell the other students in your group what you found out. Make notes about what they tell you.

3 Use your notes to write a paragraph about teenagers from different countries.

WB 31.3–5

UNIT 32

1 Skills Focus: Reading

Before you read the newspaper article, do exercises 1–3.

1 Look at the headline, 'Playing with fire in the north frontier'. What do you think the article is about?

2 Imagine that you live in a country where there is civil unrest. How would your life be different in such a country? Make a list of the differences.

3 In groups, discuss these questions.

1 What are the causes of civil unrest?
2 What are the alternatives for people who live in a country where there is civil unrest?
3 What would *you* do if you lived in such a country?

4 Now read the text. The author describes three alternatives for people living in a country where there is civil unrest. What are they?

5 Find these words in the text and underline them.

seaside resort   road junction   grannies   prams
blew up   get hurt   spattered   bits   bullets
kneecapped   drums   stick   grave   victim   misses

Discuss the meanings of the words with another student and write translations. Compare translations with two other students.

6 Read the text again. Find the paragraph in which the author

1 talks about the alternatives open to people who live in Ulster. _____
2 talks about being a victim in Ulster. _____
3 describes people's reactions to the bomb exploding. _____
4 describes his town. _____
5 describes the scene after the explosion.

_____

6 talks about how a young person can join one of the sides in the conflict. _____
7 explains how the local people know which side is responsible for a bombing or a kneecapping. _____

46

Playing with fire in the north frontier

● I LIVE in a seaside resort in Northern Ireland which isn't much different from a seaside resort anywhere else. It is a summer place, with discos and amusement arcades and go-karts and windsurfing and four miles of beach and 17 varieties of icecream to eat in the sun. The icecream shop, complete with nodding mannikin, is near a busy road junction, where kids and grannies with prams and courting couples sit on the promenade walls looking at the sea, and each other.

That's where the car blew up.

One minute Kentucky Fries, the next boom. The kid from our house, working in the icecream shop for her holiday money, didn't get hurt. Mercifully, nobody did, except the bombers, but the Kentucky Fried Chicken eaters on the promenade wall were spattered with blood and bits. Bits of dead people that is, not chickens. The chickens were dead to begin with.

It caused a bit of excitement, then it was forgotten about, like the other bombs, and the other bullets. Not the sort of thing that happens every day, but not unusual either.

When the bombs go off — or the 15-year-old gets kneecapped down an alley — we all know whodunit. The BBC doesn't have to make an announcement. It's all in the names and the places. The school you go to, the games you play, the street where you live. Everybody knows which side you're on without having to think about it.

Most kids don't go around petrol bombing or banging drums or

MARTIN WADDELL says how it is in his Ulster home

kneecapping but the game is there if you want to join in. You too can be a hero. Joining isn't difficult. You get glory and a gun and a free set of slogans to stick on your grave with colour options; red, white and blue, or green, white and gold.

If you don't want to be a hero, you can be a victim instead. If you want to be a victim you just go around doing the things kids do anywhere but you keep your head down and your mouth shut and hope that the next time the game starts it won't be your mum or your dad or your cousin or your auntie or the teacher you had in junior school who is piggy in the middle. Most of all you hope it won't be you.

You keep on going because you have to but you know that later there will be an alternative. When you grow old enough, you can leave. It's either leave, or choose which you want to be: a hero or a victim.

The kid from our house picked up her holiday money from the icecream shop and went. Now she misses home. That's the way it is over here.

● Martin Waddell won the Other Prize for his novel Starry Night, written under his pen-name of Catherine Sefton (Hamish Hamilton, £5.95). Some years ago Martin was blown up by a bomb, losing five years' work as a result.

From the *Guardian*, 1 October 1986

2 Skills Focus: Listening

104 **1 Look at the map. Listen to Denis talking about the geography of Ireland. Mark on the map**

1 the border between the Republic of Ireland and Northern Ireland.
2 the names of these towns and cities.

Enniskillin Belfast Armagh Omagh Derry

2 Listen to the next part of the interview with Denis. Match the dates and events in the history of Ireland.

1608	Anglo-Irish Agreement
17th century	British Army sent to Northern Ireland
1801	Partition of Ireland
1848	Civil War
1916	Battle of the Boyne
1916–1921	Feinian Rising
1921–1922	Plantation of Ulster
1922	Civil Rights marches
1968	Easter Rising
1969	War of Independence
47 1985	Act of Union

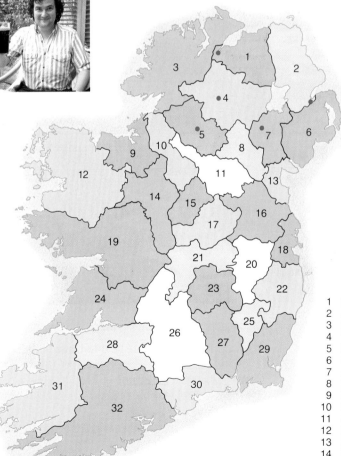

1	Londonderry	17	West Meath
2	Antrim	18	Dublin
3	Donegal	19	Galway
4	Tyrone	20	Kildare
5	Fermanagh	21	Offaly
6	Down	22	Wicklow
7	Armagh	23	Laois
8	Monaghan	24	Clare
9	Sligo	25	Carlow
10	Leitrim	26	Tipperary
11	Cavan	27	Kilkenny
12	Mayo	28	Limerick
13	Louth	29	Wexford
14	Roscommon	30	Waterford
15	Longford	31	Kerry
16	Meath	32	Cork

3 Vocabulary Development

Lexical sets

It is often useful to group words in a vocabulary book according to topic. This helps when you are writing a composition because you can look up a set of words related to your subject. You extend your vocabulary as you find other words to add to your sets, which can be divided into nouns, verbs and adjectives.

The lexical set below includes items for the composition in Unit 35.

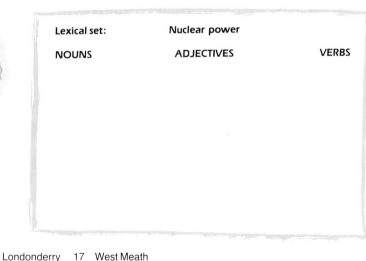

Lexical set:	Camping holiday	
NOUNS	**ADJECTIVES**	**VERBS**
comforts	free	wear
campsite	relaxed	stay
tent	overcrowded	pitch
caravan	dirty	enjoy
place	peaceful	cook
facilities	safe	sleep
gas	wet	play
rucksack		swim
sleeping bag		

Fill in the chart below with all the words you can think of connected with nuclear power.

Lexical set:	Nuclear power	
NOUNS	**ADJECTIVES**	**VERBS**

WB 32.1–4

🎧 105 Listen. **I WISH I LOOKED LIKE TOM CRUISE !**

Discuss these questions in pairs.

1 What do you think Sue said to Dave on the phone?
2 Will Dave see her again?
3 Why does Dave think that she doesn't like him?
4 Does Dave like Sylvia?
5 What do you think they are going to do this evening?
6 Does Dave feel the same about himself at the end as he did at the beginning?

48

1 Language Focus

I wish I wasn't so ugly.
I wish I looked like Tom Cruise.
I wish I didn't have so many spots.
I wish I didn't have such a big nose.
I wish I was tall and slim.
I wish I could play the guitar.

 Listen.

Now look at the pictures. What do these people wish? Write their wishes under the pictures.

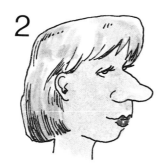

 Listen and check your answers.

2 'I wish . . .'

Look at the pictures. Make five wishes for yourself and write them down.

Example

I wish I was at the seaside.
I wish I could swim well.

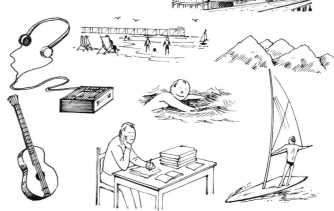

Now read your wishes to another student. Do you wish the same?

3 Wishing

 1 Look at the photographs of the four people. Listen to the conversations and find out the people's names.

2 Work in groups.

Write four wishes on separate pieces of paper. They can be about things you wish you could do or you wish you were. Don't show your wishes to the others in your group.

Fold your pieces of paper and mix all the pieces up on the desk. Take four and look at them. Read each of the wishes aloud. Give the rest of the group a chance to say whether they wish the same thing.

Example

STUDENT A I wish I was good at maths.
STUDENT B Yes, I wish I was, too. It's important.
STUDENT C I don't agree. I wish I could speak French. I think that's much more useful.

WB 33.1–2

MISTAKEN IDENTITY

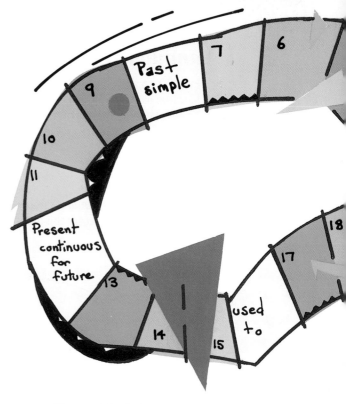

🎧 109 ▷ **Listen.**

JACKY   Good Lord! It's George Haynes, isn't it?

HENRY   Er, no, it's Henry Holmes, actually.

JACKY   Oh, yes, of course, Henry! You remember me – Jacky, Jacky Smith.

HENRY   Yes, of course I do. You used to live in Richmond, didn't you?

JACKY   No, er, it was Kingston, actually.

HENRY   Oh, yes, Kingston. Of course!

JACKY   Where are you living now?

HENRY   I'm living in Twickenham. What about you?

JACKY   In Richmond. You went to London University when you left school, didn't you?

HENRY   No, I went to Leeds. And you went to Cardiff, didn't you?

JACKY   No, Swansea, in fact. Well, anyway, where have you been working recently?

HENRY   Oh, here and there, you know. I've been working in central London for the last two years, but I'm going to work in the States soon.

JACKY   That'll be nice. What do you do now? You're a computer engineer, aren't you?

HENRY   No, I'm not. I'm a doctor. I've always been a doctor.

JACKY   Oh, yes. I remember now. And how's Doreen, your wife?

HENRY   Er . . . Doreen? I'm not married. But I'm going to get married . . . To a woman called Angela.

JACKY   Oh, that's nice. When are you getting married?

HENRY   I'm getting married next month.

JACKY   Lovely! Er, what did you say your name was?

HENRY   Henry Holmes . . . and what's your name again?

JACKY   Jacky . . . Jacky Smith.

HENRY   Actually, I don't think I know you.

JACKY   No, I don't think I know you either.

HENRY   Oh, dear . . . well . . . it's been very nice talking to you.

JACKY   Yes, wonderful to chat about old times . . .

HENRY   . . . which we haven't shared.

JACKY   Quite . . . Well, bye.

HENRY   Yes, bye.

True or false?

1 Jackie used to live in Kingston.
2 Henry is living in Twickenham now.
3 Henry went to Leeds University.
4 Jacky went to Swansea University.
5 Henry has been working in central London for the last four years.
6 Henry was once a computer engineer but now he's a doctor.
7 Henry is going to get married next month.
8 Henry and Jacky have known each other for years.

49

4 Language Focus

HENRY   You used to live in Richmond, didn't you?

JACKY   No, er, it was Kingston, actually.

JACKY   Where are you living now?

HENRY   I'm living in Twickenham.

JACKY   You went to London University when you left school, didn't you?

HENRY   No, I went to Leeds.

JACKY   Where have you been working recently?

HENRY   I've been working in central London for the last two years.

HENRY   I'm going to work in the States soon.

JACKY   That'll be nice.

JACKY   You're a computer engineer, aren't you?

HENRY   No, I'm not. I'm a doctor. I've always been a doctor.

JACKY   When are you getting married?

HENRY   I'm getting married next month.

🎧 110 ▷ **Listen.**

5 The verb tense game

This is a game for two players.

Player A Throw the dice. Move your counter the number of squares indicated by the dice. Make a sentence using the tense named on the new square. Player B decides if your sentence is correct! If it is correct, stay on the square. If not, go back to the square you were on.

Player B Now it's your turn to throw the dice.

The first player to land on the 'Finish' square is the winner!

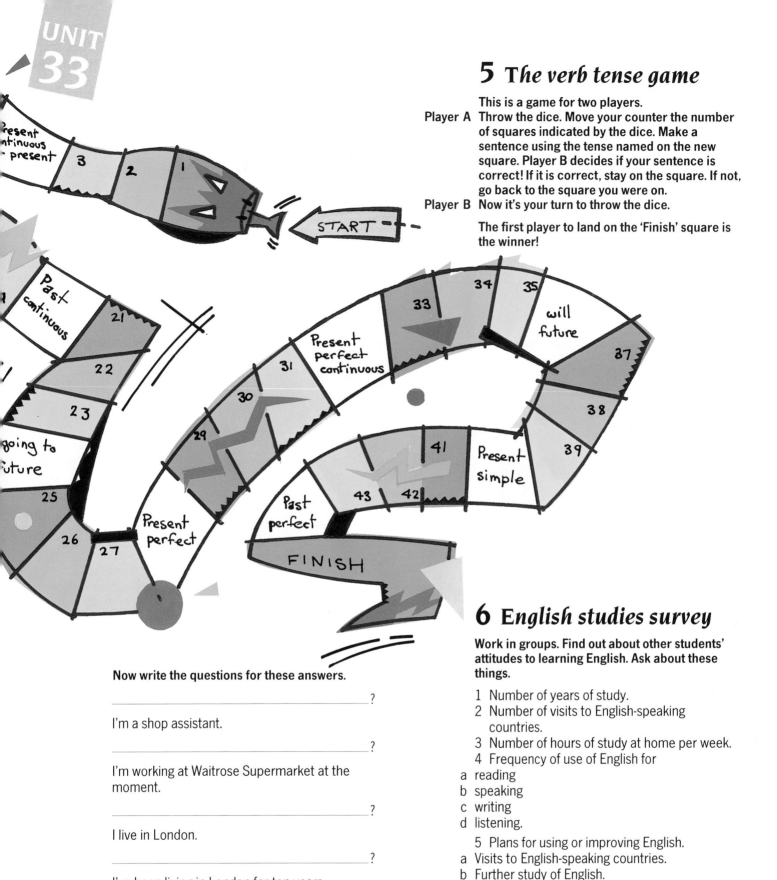

Present continuous → present
3 2 1
START →

Past continuous
21
22
23
going to future
25
26 27
Present perfect
29
30
31
Present perfect continuous
33 34 35
will future
37
38
39
Present simple
41 42
43
Past perfect
FINISH

Now write the questions for these answers.

_____ ?

I'm a shop assistant.

_____ ?

I'm working at Waitrose Supermarket at the moment.

_____ ?

I live in London.

_____ ?

I've been living in London for ten years.

_____ ?

I used to live in Bristol.

_____ ?

I'm going to Spain this year.

🎧 [111] **Listen and check your answers.**

6 English studies survey

Work in groups. Find out about other students' attitudes to learning English. Ask about these things.

1 Number of years of study.
2 Number of visits to English-speaking countries.
3 Number of hours of study at home per week.
4 Frequency of use of English for
  a reading
  b speaking
  c writing
  d listening.

5 Plans for using or improving English.
  a Visits to English-speaking countries.
  b Further study of English.
  c Use of English in a job.

Write one question for each point. Interview the members of your group.

Example

How long have you been studying English?

How often do you read English?

WB 33.3–4

MOONDOWN

Skills Focus: *Reading and Listening*

1 Before you read, discuss these questions.

1 What do you think Linda and Pete are going
to do now?
2 Do you think they will manage to save Cathy?

 112 Now listen and read.

EPISODE SEVEN

Pete and Linda are in her car
on the way to Westfield
police station.

'Come on, Pete! Tell me
what she said!'

'Sorry... She said she's a
prisoner at Moondown –
they've locked her in a room
in the basement of the ad-
ministrative buildings.'

'At Moondown! So who
met her at the pub, then?'

'It was Eastwood. He told
her that he had organised an
interview with Brooke, the
director of Moondown. He
went to the pub and then
took her to the power station.'

'But how did she manage
to phone you?'

'She climbed through a
ventilation shaft into the next
room where there was a
phone.'

'But why didn't she
escape from there?'

'She said that the door
was locked in that room,
too.'

'Then who was the
woman in the car with Jack
Sims?'

'Well... I told you we
had an informant at Moon-
down...'

'Yes.'

'Well, she worked as a
telephonist there, which is
why she knew what was
going on there... about the
dumping of the nuclear
waste, I mean. Cathy thinks
it was her in the car with
Jack Sims.'

'Poor woman!'

2 Find these words in the text and underline them.

prisoner · basement · ventilation shaft
telephonist · going on · boat load
chat · wasting · matter
calm down

Work in pairs. Discuss the meanings of the words with your partner. Write translations.

Now form new pairs. Compare translations with your new partner.

3 Put these facts from the story in order. Write *1, 2, 3,* **etc.**

____ Brooke and Eastwood locked Cathy in a room in the basement.
____ Pete told Linda about his phone conversation with Cathy.
____ Cathy phoned Pete.
____ Cathy climbed through a ventilation shaft into the next room.
____ Eastwood met Cathy at the pub.
____ Pete and Linda explained to a policeman what had happened.
____ Pete and Linda went to the police station.
▲ 50 ____ Eastwood took Cathy to Moondown.

4 Before you listen to the final part of *Moondown,* **discuss these questions.**

1 Do you think the police officer will believe Linda and Pete?
2 Do you think the police will arrest Brooke and Eastwood?
3 What do you think will happen about the nuclear waste?

WB 34.1–2

▲ 51 **Now listen and check your answers.**

113

'Yes, and they've told Cathy that she's going for a trip out to sea with the next boat load of nuclear waste tonight!'

'We'll see about that! Is this the police station?'

'Yes. Let's go in!'

'Good evening. Can I help you?'

'Yes, officer. I'm Linda Markham of the *Daily Clarion* and this is Pete Chisman of the *Westfield Gazette.* We have information about the death of Jack Sims and we know the identity of the other passenger in the car.'

'I see. Come this way, please, and we'll have a chat about it.'

'There's no time for a chat. Another person is in danger.'

'What do you mean, "in danger"?'

'She means that my col-league Cathy Edwards is a prisoner at Moondown power station and they are going to kill her tonight.'

'Er... a prisoner, sir? At Moondown? And who are "they", sir?'

'Oh dear... you're not going to believe this. The director, Mr Brooke, and the editor of the *Westfield Gazette,* Mr Eastwood.'

'It's true, officer. It may sound incredible, but it's true! We're journalists. We wouldn't be here wasting our time and your time if this wasn't true!'

'All right, madam. Now let's hear the story from the beginning.'

'We haven't got time, officer. This is a matter of life or death!'

'Yes, sir, I'm sure it is. Now, calm down a moment and tell me all about it. Now, when did this all begin?'

Skills Focus: Writing Compositions

A composition is a piece of writing which examines a particular topic. The writer introduces the topic, presents arguments for and against it, and finishes by summing up the main points and perhaps giving a personal opinion.

A good composition has four well-organised paragraphs, each with a particular purpose.

Paragraph 1 introduces the topic briefly but clearly.
Paragraph 2 presents the arguments for.
Paragraph 3 presents the arguments against.
Paragraph 4 provides the summing up.

Here are some words and phrases which are useful for introducing arguments either for or against something.

to begin with   first of all   on the one hand   particularly

As you continue, these words and phrases are also useful.

also   in addition   on the other hand   however
another point is   you can also say

When you are writing the concluding paragraph these can help.

in my opinion   to sum up   it seems to me   finally

1 Read this example of composition writing. Underline the words and phrases which present the arguments for and against camping holidays, and also those used to sum up the arguments.

Camping Holidays

More and more people go on camping holidays each year. What makes them choose to spend a period of time doing without the comforts they consider essential for the rest of the year? Why do other people find it difficult to understand what attracts them to this kind of holiday?

First of all, then, what are the advantages of a camping holiday? To begin with, people often say that they enjoy leading a life which is so different from their normal life. Also, they feel free, they can wear what they like, and they can decide from one day to the next where they want to stay. They also say that this kind of holiday is cheaper than other holidays. Families with young children, particularly, say they feel relaxed because the children can play in safety and make friends with other children on the site.

On the other hand, however, so many people go on camping holidays now that it is more and more difficult to find campsites, particularly during the school summer holidays, which are not overcrowded, noisy and dirty. Another thing is that because they are so crowded it is not, in fact, so easy to move from one campsite to another. Also, if it rains every day, they are perhaps not the best places to be.

To sum up, then, what can we say about camping holidays? They have their advantages and disadvantages like any other kind of holiday. In my opinion they are still the best kind of holiday for young people and for families with small children. Perhaps for others they are not as attractive as they were before camping became so popular. In the end, however, people must decide for themselves what kind of holiday they want.

2 Write a short composition on one of these topics. Discuss the advantages and disadvantages.

Study holidays
Living in a large family
Nuclear power

Make sure you write four paragraphs as described opposite and you use some of the language suggested for each paragraph.

1 Questionnaire: School career

Complete the questions. Ask two people in your class for their answers. Make notes.

Example

How long have you been learning English?
Would you prefer to go to university when you leave school or ...?
Do you think you have enough free time?
Do you think you have too much homework?

	Student 1	Student 2
How long have you been		
a _____ ?	_____	_____
b _____ ?	_____	_____
c _____ ?	_____	_____
What have you liked best?	_____	_____
What have you not liked at all?	_____	_____
Would you prefer to		
a _____ ?	_____	_____
b _____ ?	_____	_____
Do you think you have enough		
a _____ ?	_____	_____
b _____ ?	_____	_____
Do you have too little		
a _____ ?	_____	_____
b _____ ?	_____	_____

2 make, want, let

Write down one thing that each of these people
a **makes you do.**
b **wants you to do.**
c **lets you do.**

1 your English teacher
2 your parents
3 your best friend
4 your grandmother

In groups, read out your answers in turn. Score one point if someone makes the same comment as you. Score two points if you are the only one to make a comment.

Who made the most original statements?

3 Wishing

Write two wishes concerning each of the following.

Example

I wish my parents gave me more freedom.

1 your physical appearance
2 your personality
3 your financial position/ your possessions
4 your school
5 your home life

4 Vocabulary

These are some of the words you needed in Units 31–35. Do you know them now? Choose ten and write sentences to show you understand their meanings.

suburb	murder
illness	empty
several	ugly
suffer	prisoner
together	basement
reasonable	shot
search	matter
dead	chat

🎧 5 Pronunciation |114|

Look at these words.

1 red 2 pear
         first
         where

Listen and repeat. Listen especially to the pronunciation of the letter *r* in each case.

Now look at these words and decide which category they belong to. Write *1* or *2*.

answer ____	street ____
foreign ____	car ____
there ____	real ____
fire ____	tree ____
tired ____	here ____
scream ____	learn ____
near ____	door ____

Listen and check your answers.
Can you form a rule for when British English pronounces the *r* sound?

GRAMMAR FOCUS

How do you do these things in English? Write a sentence for each function.

1 Tell someone about something you started doing in the past and are still doing now.

_____

2 Tell someone about something your teacher obliges you to do.

_____

3 Express a wish about your financial situation.

_____

1 Present perfect continuous with for and since

a **Look at these sentences.**

How long have you been studying English?
I've been studying English for five years.
She's been living in England since she was a small girl.

b **Complete these sentences.**

How long _____ you

_____ _____ that

sweater?

I _____ _____

_____ this sweater

since the end of last month.

She _____ _____

_____ tennis for an

hour so she's very tired.

c **We can sometimes substitute the present perfect for the present perfect continuous. Which emphasises the completed action? Which emphasises** the activity which began in the past and is still continuing?
If we can use either the present perfect or the present perfect continuous with the same meaning, which do we usually use?

2 Verb + object + infinitive

a **Look at these sentences.**

She wants me to work hard.
She lets me go to the cinema every week.
She made me tidy my room.

b **Complete these sentences where necessary.**

I let her _____ borrow my

bike.

I want you _____ go to the

supermarket.

She makes her daughter

_____ stay at home in the

evenings.

c **Which of these expressions is different in form from its equivalent in your language?**
What is different about sentences with make and do from sentences with want?

3 'I wish . . .'

a **Look at these sentences.**

I wish I had a new bicycle.
I wish I wasn't so tall.

b **Complete these sentences.**

I wish I _____ more

intelligent.

I wish I _____ so many

spots.

c **Which tense do we use after wish?**
wish sentences are similar to indirect speech. What word can you insert after wish without changing the meaning of a sentence?

117

SUPPLEMENTARY EXERCISES

1 UNIT 2 *Skills Focus: Reading*

Answer the questions.

1 Why do people become au pairs, in Alison's opinion?
2 How was Alison's job different from the description on her contract?
3 In what ways was Alison's freedom limited?
4 Was Alison unhappy all the time in France?
5 Why does Alison advise people to get a job through an agency?
6 Can boys work as au pairs?

2 UNIT 2 *Skills Focus: Listening*

 Make a note of the woman's answers to Paul's questions. Try to write down her exact words.

Now work in pairs.

Student A You are Paul.
Student B You are the woman at the agency.

Act out their conversation. Try not to look at your notes.

3 UNIT 4 *Moondown: Episode 1*

 What information do you have about these people and places?

Westfield (geographical position)
         (main industry)
El Garbo (geographical position)
         (main industry)
         (cancer cases)
         (power station)
Cathy Edwards (occupation)
         (time she finishes work)
         (character)
Pete Chisman (occupation)
         (character)

4 UNIT 4 *Moondown: Episode 1*

 Complete the paragraph about the conversation between Cathy and Pete. Use these words and expressions.

Promenade Cafe   speak   important
the name   genuine   a letter   wrote
phones   convinced   article   editor
eight o'clock   Cathy   the letter
the person   meet   Moondown

Cathy _____ Pete because she has

something _____ to show him. She

arranges to _____ him at the _____

at _____. She has received _____

about _____. She doesn't know

_____ of the person who _____

_____ but she believes it is _____.

Pete is not really _____. He thinks

_____ who wrote it saw the _____ in

the *National Guardian*. _____ is going to

_____ to the _____.

5 UNIT 6 *Where's the bank?*

 Mark Sinan's route on the map. Write directions to get to the three places.

6 UNIT 6 *Looking at photographs*

 Complete the paragraph.

Bruce doesn't like the photo of

_____ because it's _____.

Jan agrees and says it's too _____. She

thinks the one of the river is _____ and

says you can't see the river _____. They

both think the one with the mountains and mist

is _____.

7 UNIT 7 *Skills Focus: Reading*

The staff at Sizewell made great efforts to present a favourable image of the power station. Make a list of the things they did to achieve this.

Example
A large clump of trees desperately tried to hide the huge white buildings.

8 UNIT 7 *Skills Focus: Listening*

 Answer the questions.

1 Sarah asks Jim Leach about the problem of nuclear waste. How does he answer her question?
2 Which industries are more dangerous than the nuclear power industry, according to Jim Leach?

3 Which other sources of power do Sarah and Jim Leach mention?
4 What does Jim Leach say about these power sources?
5 Which fuels could substitute for nuclear fuel, in Jim Leach's opinion?
6 What is the disadvantage of using these fuels?
7 What is done about the danger of melt-down in nuclear power stations?

9 UNIT 8 *Break away!*

Read the text again, then without looking at the text complete the exercise.

1 Teenagers are becoming independent at a younger age. Name two things they are doing that prove this.
2 More teenagers are spending their holidays abroad. Name three kinds of holiday that are popular.
3 Travel has become cheaper. Name two ways in which teenagers can travel more cheaply.
4 Young people often leave home before they are twenty. Name two reasons why.

10 UNIT 8 *Who can cycle faster?*

Make true sentences.

1 Wendy can't _____ as far as

_____ .

2 George takes _____ to run _____ .

3 Alice takes the _____ time to cycle 30 kilometres.

4 Ann can _____ further than _____ .

5 Alice can _____ the _____

distance.

6 Sid can _____ 30 kilometres in the

_____ time.

7 George is very _____ at running.

8 Ann _____ 10 kilometres in the

_____ time.

11 UNIT 9 *Moondown: Episode 2*

▮ 25 ▮ Answer the questions.

1 What is Frank and Alan's reaction to the letter in the paper about Moondown?
2 Do they believe the information in the letter?

3 Why does Alan believe it?
4 What do they decide to do?
5 Who phoned Cathy that evening?
6 Where are they dumping nuclear waste?
7 Why is Pete alarmed?
8 When do they dump the waste?
9 What is the time and date of the next dumping?
10 Why is Pete worried about going to Star Point?

12 UNIT 9 *Moondown: Episode 2*

 ▮ 24 ▮ Write a short summary (50 words maximum) of the episode in the past tense. Don't forget these ▮ 25 ▮ important points.

Cathy's interview with Mr Eastwood.
Cathy's talk with Pete outside Mr Eastwood's office.
The conversation that Pete hears in the pub between Alan and Frank.
Cathy and Pete's discussion about Star Point.

13 UNIT 11 *Spending habits in Britain*

Can you explain what these words and expressions mean?

1 fashions in spending habits
2 fashions in clothes
3 keep up with the Joneses
4 entertainment
5 household equipment

14 UNIT 11 *John Nutting: motorcycle journalist*

▮ 30 ▮ Answer the questions.

1 What are John Nutting's two main interests?
2 Where does he live?
3 What did he study at university?
4 Name two motorcycle magazines that John has worked for.
5 How do we know John Nutting likes his work?

15 UNIT 12 *Skills Focus: Reading*

True or false?

1 Sir Richard made *Cry Freedom* in South Africa.
2 He thinks people in the apartheid camps have lost their human dignity.
3 The South African government killed Steve Biko.

4 South Africans believe that Sir Richard is a communist.
5 The African National Congress is against apartheid.
6 Sir Richard has given part of the profit from his film to the Waterford Kamhulaba School.
7 European students cannot attend the Waterford Kamhulaba School.
8 The standard of education at the Waterford Kamhulaba School is higher than that at South African schools.
9 Desmond Tutu and Nelson and Winnie Mandela are South African.
10 Sir Richard believes that all races are equal.

16 UNIT 12 *Skills Focus: Listening*

🎧 33 **Answer the questions.**

1 Who are more numerous in South Africa – blacks or whites?
2 How often does a black man see his wife and family when he lives in a work camp?
3 What does Sir Richard say about black people's right to go into public parks?
4 What does he say about career opportunities for black people?
5 Where do black people have to live?
6 What does Sir Richard find particularly disgusting and unbelievable?
7 What does the 1948 law state?

17 UNIT 13 *War on Want*

🎧 34 **Jane, Mike or Tom?**

1 Who saw the advertisement in the newspaper?
2 Who suggests a Bring and Buy sale?
3 Who is going to church in the evening?
4 Who is going to make the posters?
5 Who is going to speak to the others in the class?

18 UNIT 14 *Moondown: Episode 3*

🎧 39 **Answer the questions.**

1 Why is Cathy waiting for Pete at the beginning of the episode?
2 Why is Pete late?
3 What do you find out about Pete's parents in this episode?
4 Why didn't Pete tell his mother about his appointment with Cathy?
5 Explain why Pete has binoculars, a cassette recorder, a torch and a radio.

19 UNIT 14 *Moondown: Episode 3*

🎧 39 **True or false?**

1 Pete was in a romantic mood when they arrived at Star Point.
2 The lorries were already at the harbour when Cathy and Pete arrived.
3 The lorries were carrying radioactive material.
4 Pete took a photo of the lorries.
5 Cathy was angry with Pete.
6 A man saw Cathy and Pete.
7 Cathy and Pete ran after the men.

20 UNIT 14 *Moondown: Episode 3*

🎧 40 **Answer the questions.**

1 Why was it difficult for Pete to run?
2 Why did the man catch Pete?
3 Did Pete know the man?
4 How did he know him?
5 Did the man believe Pete's explanation?
6 What did Pete give the man?
7 Why was Pete annoyed with Cathy?
8 Why didn't Cathy come back to help Pete?
9 Why was Cathy pleased at the end?

21 UNIT 16 *Guide to the galaxy*

Answer the questions.

1 How often can people observe Halley's Comet?
2 Name three spacecraft which approached the comet in 1985–86.
3 What did Pioneer Venus Orbiter find out about the tail of the comet?
4 Why can the comet only survive for another 1,000 orbits?
5 When will we next be able to see the comet?

22 UNIT 16 *I used to live in Italy*

🎧 45 **Complete the paragraph.**

Jane's mum went to school in _____ . She had a lot of _____ every day and she also had to do it in a _____ _____ . She had more _____ to study than Jane, too – about _____ . She did quite a lot of things in the afternoon. She went to the _____ _____ and she also had _____ lessons in the afternoon.

23 UNIT 17   *Skills Focus:* **Reading**

Underline the important sentences in the article. Use these to write a short summary (50 words maximum) of the article.

24 UNIT 17   *Skills Focus:* **Listening**

🎧 49 ▶ **True of false?**

Fionnoula says that
1 men can safely drink more alcohol than women.
2 half a pint of beer is as strong as a measure of whisky.
3 people who drink and drive have an alcohol problem.
4 people often drink because they are not confident.
5 most alcoholics are very young.
6 the number of people visiting her centre is increasing.
7 drinking to excess is mainly a man's problem.
8 they encourage everyone who goes to the centre to stop drinking completely.

25 UNIT 18   *Fed up!*

🎧 50 ▶ **True or false?**

1 Pam is in Peter's class at school.
2 Peter is tired because he has too much homework.
3 Peter wants more students in his class.
4 Peter criticises the teachers in his school.
5 Peter is tired because he plays too much tennis.
6 Peter has difficulty finding a tennis court free when he wants to play.
7 The school hasn't got enough money to build more tennis courts.
8 Peter is leaving the school at the end of the year.

26 UNIT 18   *The history of hi-fi*

Complete the sentences.

1 Louis Armstrong made his first recording on

_____ .

2 The Beatles recorded their first songs on

_____ .

3 Cassette recorders were first shown at the

_____ _____ in 1963.

4 Compact discs have a long life because

there is no direct _____ _____ .

5 DAT is going to revolutionise _____

_____ .

27 UNIT 19   *Moondown:* **Episode 4**

🎧 57 ▶ **Answer the questions.**

1 What time is it when Cathy and Pete leave Star Point?
2 Who is driving the car?
3 Who notices the following car first?
4 Does Pete think that Cathy is a safe driver?
5 What type of car follows them?
6 What colour is it?
7 Why isn't Pete tired any more?

28 UNIT 19   *Moondown:* **Episode 4**

🎧 58 ▶ **Finish these sentences to make a summary of the story.**

On Monday morning Mr Eastwood spoke _____

_____

Later, Cathy and Pete _____

_____

Mr Eastwood _____

_____

They were _____

_____

Cathy was _____

_____

Cathy and Pete went _____

_____

When they got there, _____

_____

There was a terrible mess and _____

_____

The message said _____

_____

Cathy and Pete decided _____

_____

29 UNIT 21   *You've got to do something!*

🎧 61 ▶ **Answer the questions.**

1 Who were the jeans for?
2 Did Janet give them to her brother?

3 When did she buy them?
4 What are her two main complaints about the jeans?
5 How did Janet wash the jeans?
6 What do you think the manager will do?

30 UNIT 21 *Madonna*

Close your books and write a sentence about Madonna and each of the following.

1 1959
2 *Like a Virgin*
3 1965
4 1982
5 *Into the Groove*
6 *Desperately Seeking Susan*

31 UNIT 22 *Skills Focus: Reading*

Answer the questions.

1 Which country is the worst polluter of European air?
2 Has this country's government done anything about the problem?
3 How does aluminium get into drinking water?
4 Why is aluminium pollution of drinking water a problem?
5 How does acid rain kill trees?
6 What proportion of trees is affected by acid rain?
7 What is the name of the company that produces most pollution in Europe?
8 Does sulphur from Selby cause more problems in Britain or in the rest of Europe?
9 Is Britain a member of the European sulphur emissions club?
10 Is Britain's membership important for the club's success?

32 UNIT 22 *Skills Focus: Listening*

🎧 69 **Answer the questions.**

1 Which oxides combine to form acid rain?
2 What is the effect of acid rain on rivers, lakes and streams?
3 Is all damage to trees and forests caused by acid rain?
4 What can the government do to reduce the amount of acid rain?
5 What's the problem with this solution?
6 What else have other EEC countries and North America done about acid rain?
7 Why is international legislation necessary?

33 UNIT 23 *Close encounters?*

Read the article again. Write a sentence about each of these things.

Example
January 1987
The document about the UFOs was declassified in January 1987.

1 Majestic 12
2 24th June 1947
3 Roswell Army Air Base
4 7th July 1947
5 19th September 1947
6 General Twining

34 UNIT 24 *Moondown: Episode 5*

🎧 77 Jack Sims says that the director asked to see him on Monday morning. What do you think the director said to him? What questions do you think he asked Jack? What do you think Jack replied?

Write your version of Jack's conversation with the director of Moondown. Begin like this:

DIRECTOR *Good morning, Mr Sims. Sit down.*
JACK *Thank you, sir.*

35 UNIT 24 *Moondown: Episode 5*

🎧 77 Look at this list of important details from Episode 5. Use it to write a summary of the
🎧 78 episode.

Cathy's visit to Pete – the photographs
Cathy's intentions regarding the photographs
Pete's visit to Jack Sims – Jack's interview with the director
Pete waiting for Cathy at 1 o'clock
Cathy's phone call to Pete – the informant's phone call to Cathy
Pete and Cathy's appointment – Pete's conversation with the barman
Pete's worries

36 UNIT 26 *What happened to you?*

🎧 80 **Complete the sentences.**

1 Carol hasn't got _____.

2 Bob didn't know how to get to _____.

3 Bob and Barbara met at _____.

4 The woman was running out of _____

   _____.

5 Bob and Barbara spent two hours at _____

   _____.

6 It was ten o'clock when _____

_____ .

37 UNIT 26   *Leave this to me!*

🎧 84 **Complete the conversation between Jo and Dave's mum.**

JO Hello, can I speak to Dave, please? This is Mrs Plane.

DAVE'S MUM _____

JO Can I leave a message?

DAVE'S MUM _____

JO Thank you. My daughter, Sue, was meeting Dave this evening.

DAVE'S MUM _____

JO Well, I'm afraid Sue says she can't come.

DAVE'S MUM _____

JO She says she's got too much homework and she says she's not feeling very well either – she says she had a very hard day at school today.

DAVE'S MUM _____

JO And she says she'll speak to him tomorrow. Have you got that?

DAVE'S MUM _____

JO Thank you.

DAVE'S MUM _____

JO Bye.

38 UNIT 27   *Skills Focus: Reading*

Write a history of women's football in England. Use these dates as a guide.

1921   1966   1969   1970   1971   1972

Begin like this:

In 1921 the Football Association banned women . . .

39 UNIT 27   *Skills Focus: Listening*

🎧 88 **True or false?**

1 Michelle liked dolls when she was a child.
2 Michelle is a versatile player.
3 Michelle has played football in many different countries.
4 Michelle has got a contract with Naples women's team at the moment.

5 Michelle went to the training sessions that she mentions with a group of friends.
6 She wasn't good enough to play in the match at the end of these sessions.
7 Michelle doesn't feel she's an aggressive footballer.

40 UNIT 28   *The Royal Family*

Match the people and the percentages.

34%   Girls interested in the royal family.
24%   People who thought that Prince Charles was hardworking.
22%   People who thought the royal family were ambassadors for Britain.
52%   People who thought the royal family were national symbols.
29%   People who wanted the royal family to change.
5%   People who thought that Princess Margaret was lazy.
9%   Boys interested in the royal family.

41 UNIT 28   *First aid*

Complete the paragraph.

First aid is the _____ given to people suffering from _____ or sudden _____ . It is often given by people with no medical _____ . If you know what to do you might save someone's _____ . The British Red Cross Society runs _____ in many parts of Britain to help _____ learn what to do in an _____ .

42 UNIT 29   *Moondown: Episode 6*

🎧 96 **Look at Pete's conversation with Linda Markham. Imagine what she is saying and write the complete conversation. Begin like this:**

PETE *Hello, the* Daily Clarion?
DC *Yes, that's right.*

43 UNIT 29   *Moondown: Episode 6*

🎧 97 **Pete tells the story of their investigations so far. Imagine you are Pete. Tell the story, beginning like this:**

A woman who works at Moondown phoned Cathy one day and told her that . . .

44 UNIT 31 *Diego Armando Maradona*

Read the text again, then write sentences about Maradona using these words.

1 back streets
2 outstanding talent
3 seasons
4 injury
5 championship tables
6 brilliant

45 UNIT 31 *Plans for the end-of-term party*

 What do Karen, Stuart and Julie say? Match items from the three columns to make six sentences.

Example

| *Karen says,* | *'We can ask David's mum* | *to speak to her.'* |

| Karen says,
Stuart says,
Julie says, | 'Can't you persuade her
'She wants me
'I'll give her a ring
'I hope you can come.
'Why not?
'We can ask David's mum | this evening.'
to speak to her.'
Everybody's going.'
to look after my brother.'
as it's the end of term?'
It'll be fun.' |

46 UNIT 32 *Skills Focus: Reading*

Read the text again and answer the questions.

1 Why does the author describe his seaside town in such detail?
2 What adjective best describes the atmosphere of the place?
3 What adjective best describes the scene after the explosion?
4 What was people's reaction to the explosion?
5 Would people in your town have the same reaction?
6 How do people in Martin's town know which side other people are on?
7 What is the significance of the 'colour options' red, white and blue or green, white and gold?
8 Are the people who decide to leave Northern Ireland happy after they have left?
9 Why do you think the author decided to write about the bomb explosion?

47 UNIT 32 *Skills Focus: Listening*

104 **Answer the questions.**

1 Where is Denis from?
2 When did he leave Ireland?
3 Why did he leave?
4 What are Denis's feelings about the British presence in Northern Ireland?
5 What are the names of the groups involved in the fighting?
6 In Denis's opinion, what is going to happen in Northern Ireland?

48 UNIT 33 *I wish I looked like Tom Cruise*

105 **Complete Dave's conversation with Sylvia.**

DAVE Hello, Dave here.

SYLVIA _____

DAVE Oh, hello Sylvia. How are you?

SYLVIA _____

DAVE Yes, I'm fine.

SYLVIA _____

DAVE This evening? No, I'm not.

SYLVIA _____

DAVE Yes, great, I'd love to.

SYLVIA _____

DAVE What time shall we meet?

SYLVIA _____

DAVE OK, eight o'clock outside the cinema.

SYLVIA _____

DAVE Bye!

49 UNIT 33 *Mistaken identity*

109 **Write questions about Jacky and Henry using these tenses.**

1 Present simple
2 Present continuous
3 Simple past
4 Present perfect
5 Present perfect continuous
6 *used to*

Ask another student your questions. Answer his or hers.

124

50 UNIT 34 *Moondown: Episode 7*

🎧 (112) **Think about the previous episodes of *Moondown*. Do you remember what has happened? If necessary re-read some of the episodes. Make notes about these things.**

The main characters – their names and jobs.
The main events in each episode.

Use your notes to write a summary of the story.

51 UNIT 34 *Moondown: Episode 7*

🎧 (113) **True or false?**

1 The police arrested Brooke and Eastwood.
2 Cathy Edwards was killed before the police got to Moondown.
3 Brooke had ordered the dumping of nuclear waste in the sea.
4 A policeman was shot during the arrest at Moondown.
5 The telephonist at Moondown was called Jane Cummings.
6 Jack Sims's car accident happened because the brakes failed.
7 Brooke and Eastwood have been accused of murdering Jack Sims.
8 The government is going to investigate the dumping of nuclear waste from Moondown.